GRIT & grace

SUZANNE HADLEY
GOSSELIN

—

GRETTA KENNEDY

HARVEST HOUSE PUBLISHERS
EUGENE, OREGON

Grit and Grace

Copyright © 2019 Suzanne Hadley Gosselin and Gretta Kennedy
Published by Harvest House Publishers
Eugene, Oregon 97408
www.harvesthousepublishers.com

ISBN 978-0-7369-7624-4 (pbk.)
ISBN 978-0-7369-7625-1 (eBook)

Library of Congress Cataloging-in-Publication Data

Names: Gosselin, Suzanne Hadley, author. | Kennedy, Gretta, author.
Title: Grit and grace / Suzanne Hadley Gosselin and Gretta Kennedy.
Description: Eugene, Oregon : Harvest House Publishers, [2018] Identifiers: LCCN 2018037101 (print) | LCCN 2018045296 (ebook) | ISBN
   9780736976251 (ebook) | ISBN 9780736976244 (trade)
Subjects: LCSH: Mothers--Prayers and devotions. | Motherhood--Religious
   aspects--Christianity.
Classification: LCC BV4847 (ebook) | LCC BV4847 .G67 2018 (print) | DDC
   242/.6431--dc23
LC record available at https://lccn.loc.gov/2018037101

Printed in the United States of America

18 19 20 21 22 23 24 25 26 27 / BP-SK / 10 9 8 7 6 5 4 3 2 1

Contents

To my mom, Judy,
who showed me how to be a warrior mama
by loving fiercely and pointing me to Jesus.

———— *Suzanne* ————

To my own warrior mama, Sarah,
God's generous gift to me of faithfulness,
gentleness, service, and peace.
———— *Gretta* ————

Grit and Grace

—— *Suzanne* ——

I was having one of those mornings. I was responsible for getting my infant and two toddlers to church by 10:45 so I could watch my children's pastor husband baptize kids during the morning service. Hours after my husband, Kevin, headed off to church, I was feverishly buckling my littles into their car seats (i.e., torture devices for mamas).

I pulled into church five minutes late, which meant parking in a distant spot at our large campus. As I pushed the stroller precariously through the parking lot with two toddlers in tow and a steady stream of cars driving by, I realized something: This mom thing was *hard*.

Really hard.

I mean, how did other women do this?! And how did they seem to *like* doing it?

As I burst through the door of the early childhood building looking as disheveled as a tumbleweed in a hurricane, a volunteer took one look at my welled-up eyes and asked, "Do you need help?" The floodgates opened as I explained that I just wanted to make it into service in time to see the baptisms. She kindly traded me a tissue for my stroller and whisked away my littles to their classrooms.

I sniffled all the way to the sanctuary, where I slipped into a random seat near the back, weepy and defeated. I had made it just in time, but

I felt anything but triumphant. I was *so* not rocking this mom thing. And I felt like I was the only one.

Maybe you've been there. I think we all ask ourselves versions of the same questions: *Am I good enough? Am I doing this right? Is every other mom doing this better than I am?*

Before I had children, I felt like a successful adult. I had my moments, of course, but for the most part I felt proud of my accomplishments and confident in my ability to "adult." Children changed that. I recently saw a meme that read, "I used to be the best parent in the world. That was before I had children." How true!

I remember having idealistic talks with my husband while we were dating about how we would parent our future kids. We were so sweetly naïve as we pictured an orderly home with obedient children. I pictured myself as the mom who would do it all. I would look great while offering my young children stimulating activities and play dates. I would have the house clean and nutritious dinners on the table when my husband arrived home from work. I would write from home—steaming coffee in my hipster mug—while my children played quietly (and cooperatively) nearby. How hard could it be, right?

Think back to your own imaginings of motherhood. Did you have similar ideas? How did those work out for you? Probably not exactly how you expected.

As you can probably guess, the beautiful images I had in my head didn't materialize. The reality was much, much different. It was still beautiful, in a chaotic and unpredictable sort of way. Baby cuddles on lazy mornings. Witnessing the absolute wonder of a child's curious, developing mind. Oh, and there was coffee. So much coffee. Just not always steaming and enjoyed in leisure—more like gulped down in desperation and rediscovered as "iced coffee" hours later.

With each child born—four in six years—the pressures mounted. And the more mom tasks I had to manage, the less competent and capable I felt. In fact, many days I seriously wondered if I was cut out for this. (My husband was good to point out it was a little late to be asking that question.)

As I was stretched in every way possible and pushed to my breaking point over and over again, I struggled with the identity shift from fully functional, respectable adult to the overwhelmed, insecure hot mess I had become.

Even my spiritual life took a hit. I had enjoyed a steady walk with the Lord since I put my trust in Him as a child. I attended Bible college (where I met my coauthor, Gretta). Then I worked at a Christian ministry for ten years, where I was consistently influenced by great people of faith. But connecting with God as a busy mom proved to be more difficult than I expected.

As the season of young children wore on, I began to feel more and more spiritually depleted. I blamed myself, of course. I lacked the discipline to wake up early each morning and do my Bible reading. (Never mind that I'd woken up three times in the middle of the night to tend to the baby.) But regardless of what was causing the slump, I found myself in the most demanding season of my life with very little spiritual sustenance.

To make matters worse, I felt like all my shortcomings as a mom—a lack of patience, selfish tendencies, angry outbursts—stemmed from the fact that I was not spiritually nourished and connected to the True Vine. But I only had myself to blame! I was the one who failed repeatedly to "get it together."

The more disconnected I felt, the harder it was to see the bigger picture of who God was calling me to be as a mom. He had called me, and my husband, to raise godly children who would faithfully serve Him. God describes children as arrows (Psalm 127:4). The idea is that parents get to launch those arrows out into the world to accomplish things they themselves never could. That's a *big* deal—and something the enemy wants us moms to forget. We are raising glory ambassadors who will show the world Jesus' love.

In the daily grind of changing diapers, folding endless loads of laundry, and cutting the crusts off peanut butter sandwiches, I was losing sight of that high calling. I needed a reminder of who I was—something I felt like I had pretty much figured out before I had children. Now the game had changed, and I had to rediscover who I was as a mother and still as a beloved daughter of the King.

If you can relate to what I'm saying, this devotional book is for you. A turning point for me was giving myself grace and just trying to do "something" each day, even if it was just reading one or two verses in my Bible. I needed easily accessible nuggets of spiritual truth to fortify me in the daily grind and remind me of my true identity. I also had to tell myself the truth: *Being a mom to young children is hard.* Even the most organized among us deal with insecurities as we compare ourselves to what we perceive to be the supermoms around us. But we are in this together, and we are up for the challenge. How do I know? Because God said that He preordained good works for us to do, and being a mom is one of those good works.

We need Jesus—arguably more than we ever have. We also need a lot of grit and grace. This book is written by two moms—one in the trenches of raising young children and one just on the other side—who love Jesus and believe in the powerful purpose of motherhood. Like any spiritual calling, moms can expect attacks from an enemy who doesn't want them to succeed. The good news is, we *are* more than conquerors! As we put on spiritual armor to do battle among the spilled Cheerios, splashed-in toilets, and total exhaustion of our children's little years, we can and will prevail! As we embrace who God has made us to be in this season, we can draw from resources deep within that He ordained from before the foundation of the world. This journey will not only change our children's lives; it will change ours.

1

Teach Me to Number My (Mommy) Days

—— *Suzanne* ——

My five-year-old loves to play this game with her younger sister.

"Amelia, when I'm seven, you'll be five. And when I'm ten, you'll be eight. And…Mom, how old will she be when I'm fifteen?"

I gulp. "Thirteen." I try not to panic or melt down, picturing my little girls as teenagers and realizing how quickly they will get there. In the pressures and hard work of mom life, I sometimes forget to pause and remember that this season is limited. It will come to an end sooner than I can imagine. We get approximately 936 weeks from the time our child is born to the time he or she leaves home.* That means I have about 667 weeks left with my kindergartner in the house. *Gulp.*

I remember when my coauthor, Gretta, was in the throes of the little-kid years. I was single at the time and would visit her at her cozy home in Oregon. Toys and blocks were strewn across the living room floor, random articles of clothing along the hallway. She'd serve me a tuna melt and carrot sticks, multitasking as she fielded dozens of

---

* Kristen Ivy and Reggie Joiner, *Parenting Your Kindergartner* (Cumming, GA: Orange Publishers, 2017), 11.

questions and interruptions from her toddlers. I marveled at how she seemed to take it all in stride, how she patiently spoke to her young children and attended to each little need. The selflessness I saw was astounding.

Last winter Gretta and her family were driving by my town, and we met at a pancake house along the interstate. Those three once-littles sat at the booth with us, engaging me with witty conversation and tales of their road-tripping adventures. I could barely believe the little toddler with the sprout of a pigtail was now the responsible young woman before me. The boy who had attended my wedding as a grinning six-month-old now told me knock-knock jokes. Gretta, still patient and wise, could utter a calm request and enjoy instant obedience. Pregnant with my fourth child, I marveled again. This time at how time flies.

I have heard it said that in mothering the days are long and the years are short. Though they don't always feel like it, these years of mothering young children are fleeting. I recently saw one mom I know post pictures of herself and her youngsters at a theme park. "These are the best days of our lives!" she said. "I'm sure of it." As a mom who has taken her littles to a theme park, I can say that those days don't always feel like the best ones. But I believe she is right. An empty nester once told me he'd pay $10,000 to have his adult children young again for just one weekend.

The reality that your time with your little ones is limited shouldn't depress you, Mama. It should empower you. It should empower you to sit longer snuggled on the couch, reading "just one more" book. It should empower you to set aside your to-do list to watch your tutu-clad princess perform her original production for you. It should empower you to leave the dishes in the sink to go on an impromptu family adventure.

Psalm 90:12 says, "Teach us to number our days, that we may gain a heart of wisdom" (NKJV). Numbering our days leads to wisdom. When you recognize that you only have a certain number of weeks and days with your kids, you will likely be inspired to make the most of each one you're given. Soak it all in, Mama—every moment. You have been perfectly placed for such a time as this. No need to look too far into the future. Simply enjoy what will likely turn out to be the best days of your life.

———————

Lord, thank You for the gift of my children. Help me appreciate each precious moment I have with them. Teach me to number my days so that I may be a wise mommy. Help me make the most of today as I love each precious little one in my care. Amen.

2

Stolen Identity

——— Gretta ———

I lost my identity when I became a mom. I didn't notice it at first. You see, I was excited to be a mom…it was everything I had always wanted it to be. I loved this tiny baby more than I thought possible. But six months into motherhood I realized that the only thing people talked to me about was my daughter, Kaia, or how I was doing with her. All my conversations revolved around her. She became my whole world, and I lost myself.

Come to think of it, I actually lost my identity when I became a wife. As soon as Jay proposed, all interactions with my friends became about the wedding. What were my colors? Who were my bridesmaids? What did my dress look like? And once we were married, everything was about the honeymoon and setting up our lives as newlyweds. People asked when we would start a family. And every decision I made, I now had another person to consider. I was no longer single and living on my own.

Wait a second. I lost my identity once I graduated college and started my career. I was consumed with doing a good job and having others see me as responsible and capable.

Hold on. I think I see a pattern here. Like millions of people, I have been in the habit of finding my identity in what I do, who and what I

like, and what I have. You too? It's easy to do. It starts when we are little. We are told we are pretty or smart or a fast runner. And the adults
around us all seem to care about what we want to be when we grow up.
Then, when we do finally grow up, we describe ourselves in these terms.

When was the last time you introduced yourself to someone new?
What did you say? Here's my typical introduction: "Hi, I'm Gretta. I
am married with three kids, one girl and two boys. I enjoy hiking, bak-
ing, and spending time with my family." Of course the description
changes from time to time, but that's basically the gist of it.

But what would happen if we were to focus on how God describes
us rather than how we describe ourselves? What would we say? Here
are just a few of the things God says about us.

- You are loved (Zephaniah 3:17).

- You are chosen (1 Thessalonians 1:4-5).

- You are forgiven (1 John 2:12).

- You are redeemed (Colossians 1:13-14).

- You are holy (1 Peter 2:9).

- You are wonderfully made (Psalm 139:14).

- You are gifted (Romans 12:6-8).

- You are a child of God (John 1:12).

- You are an heir together with Christ (Romans 8:17).

- You are free from condemnation (Romans 8:1).

We live, relate, and serve out of our identity. If your identity is consumed solely with being a wife or a mother, what happens when you
go through a rough season with your husband or when your children
misbehave? When your circumstances or relationships change? You
may begin to wonder who you actually are, and that doubt will slowly
eat away at your core. But if you see yourself through God's unchang-
ing truth, your core identity cannot be shaken.

Read back through that list. What do you struggle with? Which of
those truths is hard to accept? Take a few moments to ask God to give

you His eyes for yourself, so that you can live and claim your true identity in Christ.

Hebrews 10:22-23 says, "Let us draw near to God with a sincere heart and with the full assurance that faith brings, having our hearts sprinkled to cleanse us from a guilty conscience and having our bodies washed with pure water. Let us hold unswervingly to the hope we profess, for he who promised is faithful."

He is faithful. And you can claim your true identity in Him!

––––––––––

Lord, teach me to center my identity on You. I struggle to
define myself and find my worth in being _____.
Please help me see what You see in me. Remind me of who
I am and the glorious identity I have in You. Amen.

3

Toilet Paper and Broken Cisterns

—— *Suzanne* ——

My oldest son has a sensory processing disorder, which means little abnormalities in his clothing or environment can throw him off. One evening when he was four, I was getting him ready for bed and I noticed a small hole on the front of his pajama shirt. All of his other pajamas were in the laundry, and I didn't want him rejecting this remaining pair, so I smiled and said, "I know how to fix it!"

I ran to the bathroom and grabbed a square of toilet paper. I ripped it down to size and slid the small piece into the hole. "Perfect," I said. The hole appeared to be filled. Josiah was satisfied and went to bed without protest. *Mom–1, Hole–0!*

Following that event, I observed something unexpected. Each time Josiah noticed a hole in his clothing or a toy, he would say, "I'll fix it!" Then he would run to the bathroom for a square of toilet paper.

One day, about two years later, I rounded the corner into the kitchen and found him sitting on the floor, trying to plug a hole in the toe of his sock with a small scrap of tissue. That's when I realized the mistake I'd made in teaching him a solution that would never work. I tried to explain that we would need to sew the hole in the sock because the tissue would just keep falling out. But despite my explanation, his belief in the power of toilet tissue persisted.

As amusing as this parenting fail may be, it reminded me of the responsibility I have as a mom to teach my children the right solutions for the problems they face. How should they respond when they are bruised by someone's hurtful words? What should they do when a relationship is damaged through sin? How should they react when they feel stressed, afraid, or out of control?

I have realized that like it or not, I'm constantly modeling the answers to these questions in the way I live my life. When I'm stressed or anxious, do I turn to the Lord in prayer or do I seek out comfort in food, binge-watching my favorite TV show, or a little retail therapy? When someone hurts me, do I badmouth that person or choose grace and self-control? When I speak harshly to my husband or children, do I hold my ground in pride or do I say I'm sorry and ask for forgiveness?

Just before the Jews were exiled to Babylon, God spoke judgment on His people through Jeremiah the prophet. In Jeremiah 2:13, He says, "My people have committed two sins: They have forsaken me, the spring of living water, and have dug their own cisterns, broken cisterns that cannot hold water."

The people's first mistake had been to stray from the true solution to their problems—God Himself, the spring of living water. Their second mistake was constructing their own false solutions that would never work. Because of this, they were far from God and headed for big trouble.

I'm guilty of this at times. And I'm sure I've taught my children many faulty ways of dealing with life's challenges. Though I deeply desire to teach them God's ways, in my own sinfulness I often show them "broken cisterns" instead. Worthless pieces of toilet paper that still leave a gaping hole. But there is hope for this imperfect mama! When I choose to look to God as the One who *is* the solution, I lead my children to the true source of life.

I don't know how long Josiah will continue to fill holes with toilet paper, but I pray that he will learn to fill his spiritual holes with an all-powerful Redeemer. I won't always know how to "fix it," but I can teach my kids to know the One who can.

Lord, thank You for being a constant source of life and hope and help. Forgive me for the times I have turned to my own worthless solutions and taught them to my children. Help me never to forsake You, the true source of life and help. As I draw near to You, may Your living water overflow into the lives of my children and show them how to handle life's difficulties. Amen.

4

Struggling to Find Joy

——— *Gretta* ———

All my life I have wanted to be a mother. My own mother, whom I greatly admire, did a great job modeling Christlike motherhood, and I looked forward to the day when I would get a turn at it. Jay and I had been married just over a year when we decided to start trying for a family. I'd never really put much thought into it. People get pregnant every day all around the world, so I expected the same to happen to me in short order.

But one month passed. Then two. Then three. Nothing. I really expected I'd be pregnant by then. Babies were being born all around me, and friends were announcing their own excitement about surprise pregnancies, but nothing was going on in my own uterus. After four months of trying passed, I got a phone call from my brother who, after discussing their desire for more children with his wife just weeks earlier, was calling to give me the good news that they were expecting baby number three. I congratulated him, saying all the encouraging things I was supposed to say, but inside I was so frustrated and hurt and confused. I was happy for them, but it was hard to rejoice with them fully when they were getting the desire of *my* heart.

I definitely was angry with God and shed a few tears. Why would He give people babies who didn't want them and withhold or delay babies to those who did? As the months passed, my heart ached more. But then I remembered a friendship of mine that had crumbled when Jay and I were dating and then engaged. My friend was unable to rejoice with me in my new relationship, and our friendship was nearly destroyed because of it. I resolved in my heart then and there that I would be different. Despite the pain, I would choose to worship God. I would find things for which I was thankful. I would rejoice in spite of my circumstances.

My circumstances were actually nothing compared to those of the Israelites during the time of Habakkuk. (How about that one for a baby name?) Wickedness abounded, there was no godly ruler, idol worship was rampant, and captivity lurked just around the corner. Pretty bleak times if you wanted to follow God.

Habakkuk spoke back and forth to God asking for help and justice, but at the very end of the book, he comes to this conclusion: "Though the fig tree does not bud and there are no grapes on the vines, though the olive crop fails and the fields produce no food, though there are no sheep in the pen and no cattle in the stalls, yet I will rejoice in the LORD, I will be joyful in God my Savior" (Habakkuk 3:17-18).

Based on the entire book, I don't think for a moment joy came easily or naturally for this prophet. But in those bleak circumstances, he made a choice to recognize what God had done and who He is, and that choice changed his outlook on his circumstances. He chose to rejoice in the Lord, to be joyful in his Savior. That's where joy is found. True, lasting joy will never be found in our circumstances or in our possessions. Those things change and fade and can be taken away. But God is the same always. His character never changes. His goodness remains. He is faithful. He is love. When you focus on those truths of God, you can choose joy no matter what.

In the end, for us, I needed fertility help to conceive both Kaia and Titus. Looking back, I am so glad I did not give in to my frustration and hurt and become bitter toward God or those around me who had what I did not. And believe me, it did not come easily or naturally for me either.

What are you facing today? Are you longing for something so badly that you cannot be joyful in your Savior? Your circumstances may be bleak. You may be in a lot of pain. But finding your joy in the Lord and ridding yourself of bitterness will always be more rewarding in the end. And with God's help, you can do it.

Lord, I'm going to be honest. It's hard to be joyful when I feel hurt, rejected, confused, and anxious. But, God, I don't want to give in to those feelings that will lead me down a bitter, resentful path. Please help me choose, as Habakkuk did, to be joyful in You. Amen.

5

(Gingerbread) Man Down

—— *Suzanne* ——

I'm always a little sad when treasures from my pre-kids' life get irreparably damaged. At least a dozen precious knick-knacks have met their end at the hands of my children (or things that fly out of those hands). Such was the case last Christmas season, when not one but two gingerbread man ornaments took a fall at the hands of my five-year-old. The ornaments had been a gift from a coworker a decade earlier, and each year as I hung the simple gingerbread men on the tree, I was reminded of the simplicity of my single years and the career I'd enjoyed before having children.

When the first one broke, I gently scolded. When the second crashed to the floor minutes later, I yelled. The carelessness was too much to bear, especially when I'd just reminded her not to touch any more of the breakable ornaments. There were tears from both of us, but we picked up the pieces—literally—and moved on.

Fast-forward two weeks. I walk to the front gate of my daughter's school to pick her up from kindergarten. It's a few days before Christmas break, and she rushes toward me with a brown paper bag decorated with a painted handprint Santa Claus. "Open it, Mommy!" she insists. So I open it right there. Inside is a ceramic gingerbread man painted with bright colors and glitter and dangling from a white ribbon. I ooh and aah appropriately, telling her how beautiful it is and how much I love it.

As we hold hands to walk back to the car, she whispers, "Mommy, it's a gingerbread man. It's even more beautiful and sparkly than the one I broke." Tears come to my eyes as I realize what her gift means. In her mind, her hand-painted treasure is much better than the ornament I lost. And it is.

In life many things get broken: relationships, dreams, health…and let's not even get started on the ornaments! Jesus knows the pain when we have to deal with broken things. He has experience with rejection and loss and grief. And yet, when things in our lives break, He promises to offer us something new and beautiful. He redeems our pain and loss. Like that sparkly gingerbread man, what He gives may look very different from what broke, but it is beautiful nonetheless. And we can trust that He will always offer us His very best.

Jesus talks about this topic in Matthew 7:11. He addresses parents, saying, "If you, then, though you are evil, know how to give good gifts to your children, how much more will your Father in heaven give good gifts to those who ask him!"

Not only does God give us good gifts, He also redeems broken things. Isaiah states that God comforts those who grieve over what has been lost and bestows on them "a crown of beauty instead of ashes" (Isaiah 61:3). With God in the picture, brokenness is not the end state of anything or anyone. All can be restored and made even better than before.

I don't know the brokenness you're dealing with today, but likely something feels damaged in your life, whether it's a relationship, a difficult circumstance, a broken past, or an unfulfilled dream. God sees you. He understands. He sent His Son into the brokenness and the mess to make all things new.

At home, I hung the gingerbread man on my tree. And I realized something: It was ten times more precious to me than the ones I lost. In the years ahead, I'm sure more sentimental objects will meet with an untimely demise. But as pristine baubles are replaced by gaudy ones made of paper and glitter, I will remember the precious truth that God gives good gifts and redeems broken things. Brokenness is never the end.

_____

Lord, You see the broken pieces of my life. Thank You for being a loving Father who gives good gifts. Help me trust You today. To trust that even when something breaks, You can restore. To trust that when a gift looks different from what I expected, You have a good plan. Thank You that brokenness is not the end and that You redeem all things. Amen.

A Different Plan

—— *Gretta* ——

I'm not a huge planner by nature. But as my due date approached with my first child, I did everything I could to prepare. My husband and I read books. We took the classes. The doula was on call, and the bags were packed. I'd written my birth plan and discussed it with my husband and the doctor. I don't think I've ever been *that* prepared for anything in my life.

When I went into labor, Jay drove me to the hospital. It was go time! That's when it happened. A few hours into labor, my doctor told me this little girl inside me would need a C-section to get out—something to do with a low heart rate and an overly stressed baby. But all I heard was, "You failed." I hadn't been in labor that long. The doula hadn't even arrived yet. I was so disappointed. A cesarean wasn't in the plan! I was supposed to have an uneventful, drug-free delivery and bring our daughter peacefully into the world.

I'm sure I was slightly irrational with all the hormones surging through my body, but in that moment all I felt was that my dream of natural childbirth was being taken away. And I had zero control. All I could do was trust my doctor—this woman I had only met nine months ago! Did she really know what was best?

As I turned to my husband with big elephant tears in my eyes, he reminded me of our childbirth teacher's words: "The end goal is a healthy mom and a healthy baby." I nodded. The reason I had a doctor was so that she could change the plan if necessary. I didn't fully understand, but in the end I chose to trust that my doctor wouldn't make this decision unless she had a valid reason.

Proverbs 16:9 says, "In their hearts humans plan their course, but the Lord establishes their steps." We make plans. We dream. We have goals for our lives and our families. But ultimately, God decides exactly what happens. We don't always get to know why God redirects our steps. The question is, do we trust God when the plan changes and we can't understand why?

As she pulled Kaia out into the bright world, my doctor exclaimed, "Oh, that's why she didn't like the contractions. She has the cord wrapped around her neck three times!" In that moment, Jay and I knew why God redirected our plan to ensure our daughter's healthy delivery. Immediately following Kaia's birth, Jay got to share some incredible first moments with his daughter. To this day, Kaia holds his finger from time to time and says, "Daddy, remember when I was born and I did this to you?"

In all things, the Creator of the universe and the Sustainer of life and breath has a good plan and a purpose. But trusting Him isn't always easy. I don't know your situation, Mama. You may be struggling with a serious health issue. Maybe you recently lost a baby through miscarriage. Perhaps your finances seem beyond hope. It can be hard to understand why God allows us to go through things like that. I may not know what you are going through, but I do know there is a God big enough to hold you through it and worthy enough for your trust. You may never know why He changed your steps, but you can believe there's a beautiful plan far beyond what you can see right now.

God, I know You've given me the ability to make wise decisions and plan. But, Lord, sometimes I get carried away and forget that You are in control and can be trusted to oversee my life. Help me when trusting seems impossible. Remind me that You determine my steps and that Your ways are always better than my own. Amen.

Unhappy Camper

—— Suzanne ——

If you want to be humbled, go camping with young children. When my husband and I got married, we intended to go camping together. We even registered for a high-end camping grill, which we received. But six months after our September marriage, we learned we were expecting our first child. So we put our dreams of outdoor adventure on hold. Eight years and four babies later. *That's* when we decided it would be a good idea to go on our church's annual camping trip, at the beach, in a tent.

This is where I learned three very important lessons.

Lesson #1: Camping with young children is taking all of the stresses of parenting at home and adding a lot more dirt and a lot less sleep. Plus, fire.

Lesson #2: Camping with young children will quickly bring you face-to-face with your control issues and inadequacies. This was made painfully obvious the first morning as I sat crying into my breakfast sandwich (lovingly brought to me by my husband after he'd had to drive our noisy children out of camp at 5 a.m.) while my three-year-old declared boisterously, hands on hips, "Well, *I'm* having fun!" (At least somebody was.)

Lesson #3: Camping with young children will make memories that none of you will ever forget (even if you would like to). The air mattress deflating in the middle of the night while you're trying to nurse the baby. Every square inch of sticky little bodies covered with dirt and sand. The ants infesting your picnic table, pillaging the scraps of peanut butter and jelly sandwiches left there the night before. And then there are the smiles. The giggles. The unbridled joy of little ones jumping into the surf, dancing in the firelight, and discovering "treasures" along the trail.

When I thought about why this camping thing made me feel so defeated, I realized it was because I was not operating within my strengths. Unlike my husband, flexibility isn't my strong suit. Let's just say I don't have the strongest track record for rolling with unforeseen challenges. I like to know exactly what's going to happen so I can feel in control. I also like to be showered and smell nice, for that matter!

I realized a lot of my struggle came down to a belief that I'm more valuable when I'm operating in my strengths...when I'm confident and feel I have something to offer. But the truth is, God can use me in my weakness too. Discomfort and even failure draw different things out of me, such as dependency on others. You would not believe how many kind souls fed my kids, said an encouraging word, or offered a hug.

Second Corinthians 12:9 contains this incredible truth: "He said to me, 'My grace is sufficient for you, for my power is made perfect in weakness.' Therefore I will boast all the more gladly about my weaknesses, so that Christ's power may rest on me."

Mama, in those moments when you are uncomfortable, and so *very* aware of your own inadequacies, God gives you more grace. He invites you to just be...weak. That's it. You don't have to be strong. You don't even have to be functional. In fact, you can brag "all the more gladly" about your weakness because it provides an opportunity for Christ's power to shine through you. People will look at your chaos and *know* there is no way you would be surviving this if not for Jesus.

I still question our judgment in attempting our first family camping trip with four children six and under. (And to tell the truth, we packed up a day early to get back to our own beds sooner.) But my children can't stop talking about going again. So I may just need to toughen up, drink more coffee, and give it another try…say, in five years.

———————

Lord, I offer You all of me today—my strengths and my weaknesses. Thank You for creating my inmost being and for Your all-sufficient grace. Work through my inadequacies and show Your power when I am weak. Remind me that You shine brightly in the very areas in which I fail to shine. Allow my frailty to draw others to You. Amen.

8

Simple Pleasures

——— *Gretta* ———

Unlike Suzanne, I love camping! In fact, when our children were young, we planned a monthlong dream camping trip in Hawaii. Everyone told us we were crazy and couldn't do it. I think they may have even questioned our sanity. But after selling our home in Oregon and before Jay started his new job as a camp director in British Columbia, Canada, we knew the time was right.

We checked our tent, cooler, sleeping bags, and camp stove onto the plane and loaded up our children—three, two, and seven months—for the adventure of a lifetime on the tropical island of Kauai. We had a lot of stuff, but somehow we managed to pack it all into three checked bags, six carry-ons, and a double stroller. It was everything we would need for the next four weeks.

Between our tent setup just feet from the beach and the rental car parked across the field, we had everything we needed. The thing I love most about camping is its simplicity. We prepare all our food on the camp stove. We have no toys apart from a bucket and shovel, a few Matchbox cars, and books. No Exersaucer or dolls. No craft supplies or child-sized hardware set. And this trip occurred before smartphones and personal tablets—so no electronics.

For an entire month we lived simply. And nearly every night as I looked at my babies snuggled in their sleeping bags and thought over the day and how they had chased tiny crabs back into their holes or splashed in the waves on the boogie board, I took a deep breath of contentedness.

Camping does something for me that few other activities do. Normally I am bombarded with stuff. Stuff to make my house pretty, stuff to keep my children happy, stuff to help me stay healthy or to make us more comfortable. But all this "stuff" takes a lot of work to acquire and to maintain. It takes finances to purchase, time to shop for or create, and then work to fix, clean, and take care of it all. All the stuff that is supposed to make life more enjoyable, easier, and fulfilling instead has the potential to create chaos and stress that can end up suffocating me.

When I'm camping I'm reminded of what's important—how little we actually need to survive. The need to consume disappears. The desire to be entertained shifts. And I refocus to see what really matters. You may think I'm crazy (I'm sure Suzanne does), but it happens every single time I go tent camping (and living on beautiful Vancouver Island, I go a lot).

When I'm camping, I see very tangibly what Proverbs is talking about when it says, "Better a little with the fear of the LORD than great wealth with turmoil" (15:16).

What's the important thing here? Is it having great wealth and comfort? That's sure the North American dream. We are led to believe that money and comfort will solve our problems. Is the important thing in this verse to have very little? To be poor and have nothing? Well, that's not really it either. Issues also come with having no money to pay the bills.

If you look closely, the verse says it's the fear of the Lord where the value lies. Having a reverence, a love, and a desire for God is what's best. And God knows it's easier to depend on Him when you have nothing than when you have the stresses that come with managing so much stuff. You see Him better. You rely on Him more. You focus better on what is important because the noise of "stuff" dissipates.

When you feel overwhelmed with the stuff of life and the turmoil of too much, maybe you need to simplify and go camping in your soul for a bit. Return to the reverence and fear of the Lord, who He is, and what He has done. Just watch. The chaos will quiet down, and you will look around your tent and realize you have everything you need right in front of you.

———————

Lord, remind me of the beauty of simplicity. I want to understand what it means to embrace having little with deep reverence for You instead of having the latest and greatest with turmoil. Give me the ability to be content with what I have and pursue You more. Amen.

9

Hope in a Hopeless Place

—— Suzanne ——

My scariest mom moment happened when my firstborn, Josiah, was seven months old.

Just under two years into marriage, Kevin and I loved being new parents. Josiah had hit each early milestone, loved to giggle and coo, and lit up our world. But in July he began showing some unusual symptoms. When I was feeding him in his high chair, his head would drop suddenly. At other times he would roll his eyes and stiffen his limbs. We took him to the doctor on a Thursday, but Josiah didn't exhibit the symptoms during the visit and the doctor sent us home.

By Saturday we knew something was definitely wrong, so we rushed our baby to the emergency room, where triage put him on oxygen and admitted him to the hospital. He was poked and prodded and scanned as Kevin and I stood by helplessly. Finally, sensors and wires were attached to his little peach fuzz head to conduct an EEG—the first of many.

The diagnosis came quickly: Our son had Infantile Spasm Syndrome, a catastrophic form of childhood epilepsy. The electrical charges in his brain were going haywire. I remember curling up on the vinyl hospital couch that night after Googling the worst-case scenario

on my phone. A fledgling mommy, I felt completely and utterly helpless. As far as we knew, our son had been developing normally, doing
fine at his six-month well check. But by the time we left the hospital,
Josiah had the motor skills of a baby half his age.

We started him on the treatment with the best prognosis. The neu-
rologist told us there was no guarantee the treatment would stop the
seizures or Josiah's developmental decline. I have never before or since
grappled more with what I truly believe. I had to release my baby's
future into God's hands, not just talk about doing it. Things had just
gotten real.

As believers, we are blessed to have access to the ultimate source
of hope in Jesus. Lamentations 3:25 says, "The LORD is good to those
whose hope is in him, to the one who seeks him." And Psalm 25:3 proclaims, "No one whose hope is in you will ever be put to shame."

After we took Josiah home from the hospital, I was overcome with
fear and dread. Many nights I woke in the middle of the night and hurried into Josiah's room to pray God's protection over my son. Trusting
God was a daily decision, and I desperately needed hope.

Josiah's seizures did stop, and little by little he began to develop
again. He learned to sit up, crawl, and finally walk. Progress was slow
but constant. And we rejoiced with each milestone. Josiah's development has not been typical, but God has been gracious. Raising this special little boy, who still loves to laugh, has taught me so many things.
One of them is that I am not in control (as much as I would like to be!).
Another is that my children are not mine; they belong to the Lord. At
times I would pick a different plan for them, but I choose to believe
that God's plans are better.

Mama, do you need hope today? You may not have a sick child, but
perhaps you have a sick relationship that needs God's healing touch.
Maybe you feel at the end of your resources and wonder how you will
keep going. God promises that His love for you is steadfast and your
confidence in Him is never misplaced. Josiah's name means "Jehovah
heals," and that is exactly what God has done in my son's life. God has
healed me too, and shown me that I can have hope in the darkest places
because He's always right by my side.

Lord, Your ways are amazing! Thank You for the way You bring hope into the darkness. I praise You for Your goodness. Help me when I want so desperately to take control. In dark moments when I can't see Your plan and I don't understand, remind me of who You are and that there is always hope. Amen.

10

Faith like a Child

—— *Gretta* ——

I think from the moment she could speak, Kaia was praying with a faith and certainty unlike any I had ever heard. We live in a very wet climate. It rains on Vancouver Island from October to June, and if it's not raining, then it looks like it's about to rain. One day we were in the car with about an hour left in our journey home and it was raining uncharacteristically hard. Kaia simply said, "Mama, I'm going to pray that it stops raining."

In my mind I thought that was a silly thing to pray because, after all, we live on Vancouver Island. But I put on my good mama voice and said, "Sure, honey. You can ask God anything. He can always hear you."

That's when I heard her from the back seat, "Dear God. Please make the rain stop and the sun come out. No more rain until we get home. Amen." In roughly ten seconds we turned off the windshield wipers and saw the sun peek through. And it didn't rain again until we pulled into our driveway an hour later! As soon as we turned off the wipers, she said with delight, "God heard me!"

Her faith just grew from there. I remember the summer Suzanne let me know that her first baby, Josiah, was in the hospital at seven months old having seizures. She was terrified because Josiah didn't seem to be responding to treatment and the prognosis for his development wasn't good. I ended a difficult and tearful phone conversation with Suzanne feeling burdened for my friend and her baby.

That night at bedtime, five-year-old Kaia noticed my sadness and asked about it. I explained Josiah's situation the best I could. Though she had never met Baby Josiah, she offered to pray for him. In her matter-of-fact, faith-as-a-child way she prayed, "Dear God, I pray for Baby Josiah's brain. Thank You for giving Him one. Help it get all better and help his mommy love You so, so much. Help Baby Josiah to not have any problems with his brain anymore. Amen." And with that, we kissed and said good night.

I know that God wants us to bring our burdens to Him, but sometimes children remind us of how simple it is. First Peter 5:7 says, "Give all your worries and cares to God, for he cares about you" (NLT). God invites us to bring our worries and cares to Him the way my daughter did—with childlike faith. In Luke 18:17, Jesus says, "I tell you the truth, anyone who doesn't receive the Kingdom of God like a child will never enter it" (NLT).

So many times it's difficult to take Philippians 4:6-7 at face value and practice it: "Don't worry about anything; instead, pray about everything. Tell God what you need, and thank him for all he has done. Then you will experience God's peace, which exceeds anything we can understand. His peace will guard your hearts and minds as you live in Christ Jesus" (NLT).

We like to complicate things, don't we? But God tells us we really don't need to. In fact, it's not His best for us. Instead, He gives us a clear guide of His design for our behavior.

1. Faith like a child.

2. Don't worry. Instead, give all your worries to God.

3. His peace will guard your heart and mind.

Isn't that freeing? Doesn't that just make you want to pray? Give God your worries and in return He will give you His peace.

Kaia was so sure Josiah would be healed she prayed for him without worry and went to sleep in peace. A few days later when I asked her if she wanted to pray for Josiah again, she looked at me quizzically. "God already healed Baby Josiah's brain," she said.

My daughter's bold, simple faith grew my own. And I believed with her that God would heal Josiah, which He did. God stopped the seizures, the medicine began to work, and Josiah has exceeded expectations in his growth and development.

It's time to let go of your worries, Mama. Stop complicating things, and simply trust like a child.

Dear God, give me faith like a child. Help me pray and truly give my worries over to You so I can stop holding on to them. Please give me the faith to believe You can do great things and give me peace as I release my cares to You. Amen.

11

Worth the Work

—— *Suzanne* ——

For Christmas last year my husband gave me a great gift. He bought us two dinners a week from a meal delivery service to give me a much-needed breather from meal planning. During those first few weeks, we feasted on street-style poblano tacos, tangy barbecue pork loin, and Parmesan chicken tenders—in other words, some of the best eating we'd done in months. Even the kids liked the simple, gourmet fare.

I only had one complaint: I still had to cook.

The boxes came with produce to wash and chop, meat to prepare, and sauces to concoct. All the ingredients were there, but Kevin and I (yes, that sweet man offered to help me) had to put in about an hour of work to get our culinary masterpiece on the table.

My disenchantment made me think about how we live in an "instant" world—mobile coffee orders, immediate information on the Internet, drive-thru everything, free overnight shipping. These things make us feel like we can have everything *now* and shouldn't have to wait. Sometimes I can adopt this same mentality with my kids. I want to see instant results in my children without putting in the work. When they drop their jackets in the middle of the floor two days (or weeks) in a row, I'm aggravated. When I tell them not to fight, I'm perplexed when future playtimes resemble a *West Side Story*–style street rumble. And when I point out misbehavior, I expect angelic behavior the next time.

The truth is, raising the next generation of Christ followers isn't an instant thing. It's a long, labor-intensive process of teaching and training through many little circumstances and situations…every day… week after week…year after year. No wonder I've been more mentally and physically exhausted being a mom than I have at any other time in my life.

The familiar parenting passage, Deuteronomy 6:5-7, says, "Love the Lord your God with all your heart and with all your soul and with all your strength. These commandments that I give you today are to be on your hearts. Impress them on your children. Talk about them when you sit at home and when you walk along the road, when you lie down and when you get up."

These were God's parenting instructions to His people, the Israelites. He told them to impress His commands on their children. Much like a cookie press that turns out perfect shortbread cookies with a beautiful design, God tells us to stamp His Word on our kids over and over again. How do we do that? The answer is surprisingly simple: Talk about it. Talk about who God is and what He says *all. The. Time.* Talk about it first thing in the morning. Talk about it last thing before bed. Talk about it at home. Talk about it pushing the cart through the grocery store. Talk about it driving home from school.

Making this kind of impression begins with me nurturing my own love for God. And after that, every moment is an opportunity to impress *Him* on my children.

This is a big task but also a doable one. The ingredients are all there— you, your children, God's Word. But it doesn't happen instantly; it takes work. It happens when I engage in real conversation with my three-year-old instead of scrolling through social media on my phone. It happens when I look for opportunities to explain how our everyday activities relate to God's purposes in the world. It happens when we read the children's Bible together at bedtime and talk about how amazing our heavenly Father is and how much He loves us.

Raising godly children doesn't happen overnight. But that's okay.

At times I'll still long for the instant results, but growing along with my children is a process. And as I take advantage of the everyday opportunities to teach my kids about God, I can trust that with His help the end result will be worth the effort.

Lord, thank You for entrusting me with this big, hard, beautiful, daunting, amazing task of introducing my child to You. Help me fight my cravings to see instant results and to instead focus on daily reinforcing Your truth on my child's heart, planting seeds in each fertile corner. Bless my humble efforts and multiply them for the building of Your kingdom. Amen.

12

Light of the World

——— *Gretta* ———

Our first home was perfect. A tiny three-bedroom rancher, 1,000 square feet all our own with a little fenced backyard, located on a quiet cul-de-sac. We moved into it in December and got to work right away setting everything up and making it ours. It wasn't until the spring that we realized how different we were from our neighbors. Every weekend we were serenaded by grown men who had clearly had too much to drink. The loud conversations, music, and semi-partying left us wondering if we made a poor choice in this new home ownership venture. One neighbor—we'll call him Tony—often enjoyed his backyard half-dressed standing at the grill or sitting in his hot tub.

As the summer wore on, however, we slowly began to initiate conversations. I have to admit, this had more to do with Tony sharing meat across the fence than it did with our enthusiasm in forming a friendship. They were not our first choice in neighbors, but we quickly realized that God had put us beside them on purpose. And once we understood that, we viewed them differently. Instead of being bothered by Tony's behavior, we looked for ways to reach out in love.

By the time Kaia was born, we were friends enough that Tony's wife, Amy, came to visit us in the hospital. Jay and Tony went fishing together. Amy and her daughter joined us at church a few times.

For the few years we shared a fence, Tony and Amy watched how we lived. They heard us talk about God several times, but never chose to follow Him while we were neighbors. They watched us welcome all three of our children into our family, and we moved to Canada shortly after Koen was born. I don't know if they ever chose to follow God, but I do know that for four years they saw us live differently from anyone they knew. During that season we realized that God wants to use us wherever we live—even if that means becoming friends with neighbors we would never choose for ourselves.

Tony once said to Jay, "You're pretty cool even if you are a Christian." If nothing else was gained from our time next door, I'd say that was pretty exceptional.

> You are the light of the world. A city on a hill cannot be hidden. Neither do people light a lamp and put it under a bowl. Instead they put it on its stand, and it gives light to everyone in the house. In the same way, let your light shine before others, that they may see your good deeds and glorify your Father in heaven (Matthew 5:14-16).

This verse says that everywhere you go, people should see something different about you. The checker at the grocery store should see that even though you may be tired from shopping with your littles, you still have kindness. Your neighbors should see you encouraging your spouse and your kids toward gentleness. The other moms at playgroup or at the park should hear you speak love over the difficult areas of your life. This behavior, of course, comes from God alone. And when you live like that, your light will shine like a city on a hill and those around you will call you "pretty cool, even though you're a Christian." Most importantly, God will be honored and glorified.

So who is your "neighbor"; whom do you need to love? Anyone difficult? Regardless of how crazy life is within the walls of your home, you are a light everywhere you go. So shine on, Mama. Shine for all to see.

Dear Lord, give me Your love, joy, patience, gentleness, and kindness to share with others. Help them see Your life in me. In how I talk, in how I discipline, and just in how I interact with life. Use me to shine brightly so that everyone will praise You and know You better. Amen.

13

Reporting for Active Duty

—— *Suzanne* ——

It was five o'clock, and I was having one of those days where there's *way* too much day left at the end of my patience. My three-year-old had recently given up her afternoon nap, which meant Mommy hadn't had a break all day. And Daddy had a dinner meeting, so there was no relief in sight.

As I prepared dinner, I surveyed the landscape of my life: As far as the eye could see, my house looked like the aftermath of a hurricane. The kids were giving Oscar-worthy dramatic performances in the family room, fighting over which cartoon they would watch next. And macaroni noodles boiled over on the stove.

As the baby wailed from his high chair (the safest place he could have been at that moment) and I considered the same course of action, a thought entered my mind: *This is* not *what I signed up for!*

I can't be the only mom who has felt that way. Whether it's managing the grueling daily tasks of being a mom, being a single parent, or ending up with a child who's medically fragile or has special needs, being a mom is not for wimps! And at times motherhood can feel like a bait and switch. You imagined it to be one way, and the reality is completely different. You imagined you'd be a certain kind of mom, and *you* are completely different. You may even wonder for an instant whether you would have taken it on had you fully known what the job would require.

In life we sign up for many things. We accept the job offer. We join the organization. We take the class. We volunteer. But the truth is that we don't sign up for motherhood. (If you're playing devil's advocate, yes, I know where babies come from—I have four children—but hear me out!) We may make a choice to bring a child into the world, but we are recruited by God to be that child's mother.

A casual look through Scripture reveals that God's purposes are very specific—bizarrely so at times. Think of how He chose a young boy with a slingshot to bring down the Philistine giant or how a fish coughed up a coin for Jesus' disciples to use to pay taxes. God uses the details. He not only knows your children; they are under your care for a reason.

When I think of it that way, it kind of changes everything. I have been recruited! I am called to *my children*. And the great news is that I'm not in this alone. First Thessalonians 5:24 says, "The one who calls you is faithful, and he will do it." And Ephesians 2:10 offers this encouraging word: "We are God's handiwork, created in Christ Jesus to do good works, which God prepared in advance for us to do."

While motherhood can seem like a monumental task, God promises to be with us every step of the way. He Himself equips us for the task. Before you were ever born, He knew the good works you would do. Good works like refilling sippy cups, finding the misplaced shoe, building a blanket fort, kissing boo-boos, and providing extra snuggles at bedtime.

Whether you're just starting your day and hoping for smooth sailing or about to finish up "one of those days" where your house looks more like a demolition site than a home, take comfort in the fact that God has recruited you. And He'll help you do all the wonderful things He has planned.

———————

Lord, I confess that sometimes I feel ill-equipped for
my job as a mom. Thank You for calling me to this

special task. In the busyness of life, help me remember that being a mom is a privilege that You ordained for me before I was ever born. When I am overwhelmed, help me rely on Your faithfulness in my life. Amen.

14

Cheerleaders in the Delivery Room

——— *Gretta* ———

When it came time for me to deliver my second child, my doctor and I decided to try for a VBAC delivery. Baby Titus was healthy, I was healthy, and there was no reason to suspect we would have any of the same issues that caused my first to be born via cesarean. I had always dreamed of delivering a child naturally, without drugs or any intervention. I claimed my reasons were because I didn't want drugs going into my baby, but if I am really honest, the true reason was that I wanted to know if I could do it. I can be a bit stubborn and willful, and I just wanted to *know* that I was mentally and physically strong enough to push out a baby on my own.

I didn't really labor with Kaia, so though Titus was my second child, this would be my first experience. I was home by myself with 19-month-old Kaia when contractions started. Jay was at work just five minutes away. As my contractions slowly increased in frequency and intensity, I slowed my breathing, concentrated on a focal point across the room, and basically tried to do everything I had been taught by my birthing coach.

Eventually I called a friend to come over and help watch Kaia so I could focus on being in labor. Not long after that, Jay returned home so together we could drive to the hospital to welcome our second child into our family.

I walked into the hospital, got my room, changed into that ever-lovely gown, and pressed on through the pain. I was progressing along quite well and knew the end was in sight, but I was realizing this just might be the toughest thing I had ever tackled. With each contraction, Jay held my hand, rubbed my back, and kept the room quiet while I focused all my energy on getting my son out.

I must admit that in the moments between contractions I began to wonder if my goal was impossible. The pain was incredible, and I was tired. But honestly, a few times I thought on how millions of women had been doing this very thing for generations. Millions of babies have been brought into the world in small huts with dirt floors and even in the middle of rice fields. In those moments, I kept thinking, *They did it, you can too.*

Admittedly, pushing an entire human out a small hole hurts like nothing else, and I am certainly not happy with Eve for sinning all those years ago, bringing the punishment of pain in childbirth to all future women. But oddly enough, knowing I was not the first woman to feel all this pain gave me encouragement. After several hours of labor and pushing like I'd never pushed before, I received the greatest reward for all that hard work. I met my son for the first time, and miraculously the pain dissipated. I still remember the hard work, but the joy of my child made it all worth it.

No one said childbirth was easy. Just like no one said living a life honoring God and obeying His guidelines would be easy (or at least I certainly hope you weren't told that), but it's definitely worth it.

Hebrews 12:1 says, "Since we are surrounded by such a great cloud of witnesses, let us throw off everything that hinders and the sin that so easily entangles. And let us run with perseverance the race marked out for us." Did you know you are surrounded by people who have done this mothering thing before you? And they've done it with excellence. They are cheering you on, encouraging you to persevere and stay the course. They are not judging you for your mistakes. No, they are cheering from the sidelines, saying, "I know it's hard, but you. Can. Do. It."

They are saying, "Breathe, and keep focused on Jesus." And, "*Persevere! The reward is great!*" It's what I'm saying and what millions who have gone before you are saying.

Your birth story is different from mine. Hey, all three of mine are different from one another! Your mothering journey will look unique to you, and your relationship with Jesus definitely has its own flavor. But what it has in common with everyone else is it takes focus, determination, perseverance, and endurance to complete it well. There are hiccups and pain along the journey, but as Hebrews tells us, we are surrounded by men and women of faith who have gone before us to let us know it can be done, and more than that, they are cheering you on even now. As you sit here, reading these words, they are cheering you on to run with perseverance. To keep your eyes focused on Jesus. It's a beautiful picture, isn't it? You have what it takes, and you *can* do this!

God, thank You for the encouragement that I have a cheering section in this mothering journey and in my faith journey with You. When I feel defeated, tired, or like I just can't keep going, bring this truth to mind and help me persevere and stay the course. Amen.

Cleaning Up the Crumbs

—— *Suzanne* ——

One day I was helping my five-year-old daughter clean the playroom when we discovered some Cheerios strewn all over the carpet.

"Pick them up right away," I told her. "Food in the carpet attracts mice."

"I like mice!" she replied. "They're so cute."

I broke the news to her that mice are dirty and carry diseases, which is why we can't have them in the house. Then I told her that we would have to set a mousetrap if any came in. She seemed excited about this prospect, until I explained how a traditional mousetrap works: You place the bait, and a metal piece snaps down and kills the mouse.

Her eyes widened in horror. "No! I don't want to do that," she said adamantly. She then described her ideal trap, which would allow the critter to live and preferably become her pet.

At an impasse as to how to deal with the hypothetical rodent problem, I finally reminded her, "Let's just pick up the cereal so that we don't have to deal with the problem."

"Okay," she agreed.

This exchange reminded me of how a little carelessness with my thoughts or actions can grow into a big sin problem. The first crumbs are often left there out of distraction or busyness, but if I don't attend to them, they attract something much more sinister.

Listen to what James 1:14-15 says about the birthing process of sin: "Each person is tempted when they are dragged away by their own evil desire and enticed. Then, after desire has conceived, it gives birth to sin; and sin, when it is full-grown, gives birth to death."

Every big sin in our lives started out as something smaller, maybe even something that seemed totally harmless, such as failing to pray about something before dealing with it in our own way or letting an inappropriate thought linger or becoming too busy to nurture an important relationship.

Like Cheerios on the ground, these careless thoughts and actions attract something dangerous—an ungodly desire that gives birth to sin, which ultimately gives birth to death.

The consequences of sin can be devastating. And when sin is full grown, we wish we didn't have to deal with it, but we must. How much heartache and hassle could be avoided if we just picked up the Cheerios? If we held our tongues before the harsh words came out? If we took that uncharitable thought captive and allowed God to replace it with right thinking? If we dealt with the conflict immediately instead of letting it grow to something unmanageable?

Mama, what crumbs are you leaving around today? Ask God to show you where thoughts and habits are laying the groundwork for sin. And if the sin has already grown and become a bigger problem, it's not too late. God promises that when we confess our sins, He is faithful and just to forgive us of *all* unrighteousness (1 John 1:9). Seek out support. You have help to sweep up the crumbs or kill the vermin of sin—that is one of the wonderful things about God's grace. Call on Him to help you today.

Lord, I confess that I sometimes get busy and distracted and allow bad habits to hang around. Help me pick up the cereal in my life before it becomes a bigger problem.

God, search my heart and reveal to me the things I'm doing that prevent me from being in right relationship with You and others. I ask forgiveness for my sin. Thank You for being faithful and just to forgive me. Amen.

16

Soo-soos

—— *Gretta* ——

Beaches have always held the perfect location for my family to relax. We were blessed with friends who owned a beach cabin and gave us our own key to use the cabin whenever we wanted. It just so happened that we wanted…often.

Our typical routine at the cabin had us playing in the sand in the morning for a few hours and returning for lunch. On one visit it's very possible that we had played a bit too long, and our tummies grumbled loudly, informing us of this fact. As I stood in the kitchen, frantically making our lunch as quickly as I could, Kaia, at 18 months, walked around the living room whining and fussing as she waited for food. She was hungry and definitely let me know.

As her grumpiness continued to grow, Jay knelt down, looked her in the eye, and said, "Kaia, say 'patience.'" I laughed at him because, well, how in the world could she say such a big word, let alone understand its meaning? But in the best way she could, she replied, "Soo-soos." Admittedly, I stifled a giggle as I often did whenever this little toddler repeated whatever we asked her to say. I mean, aren't kids adorable as they're learning to speak? But to my utter amazement, she calmed down for a few moments.

Granted, the peace only lasted a few moments, but still, she somehow knew. When she'd start getting worked up again, Jay would repeat the interaction: "Kaia, say 'patience.'" And a tiny little "soo-soos" came out of her mouth again. This cycle continued until lunch was ready.

As she grew, eventually "soo-soos" morphed into "patience," but in our family, we can still say "soo-soos" and we all know a bit of patience is needed. It's our kind way of saying "wait nicely." But waiting is hard, isn't it? Psalm 130:5 says, "I wait for the LORD, my whole being waits, and in his word I put my hope."

The concept of waiting is talked about over and over in the Bible. Every time it is mentioned, no matter what is being waited for, it comes with an attitude of expectancy or anticipation and, most notably, hope. Having patience, the kind talked about in the Bible, has more to do with your attitude than with how long you must wait. To keep an attitude of expectancy requires resting in God's character and His goodness. The hope that accompanies waiting isn't a fleeting "wish upon a star" kind of hope. Rather, it's an assurance of what is to come. God's goodness always wins out. So no matter what you are waiting for, you can be assured that God will answer according to His goodness.

You see, even at 18 months, Kaia knew I was making her lunch. She saw me working and trusted food was coming. It always did. So without realizing it, she was able to trust my character to provide her with nourishment. And that was what she needed to wait with expectation and hope.

Have you ever thought about that? Trusting in God's good character gives you the strength to hope. To wait. To be patient. It's hard to wait. What are you waiting on God for at the moment? Are you struggling with infertility? Do you have health issues in your family? As you wait for God's timing, be assured that He will answer according to His goodness. And that is your assurance that gives you hope, even if the answer isn't what you think is best. Trust God's best. And then you can be patient.

———————

God, help me rely on Your good character. As I
wait, give me the assurance needed to have patience
and hope. You are good. I trust You. Amen.

17

Love > Worry

——— Suzanne ———

I stood in church for the first time in a month. After developing a serious seizure disorder, our son Josiah had been on house arrest because of some medications that made him susceptible to other serious illnesses. As I held Kevin's hand and sang, "He loves us, oh how He loves us…" (one of my favorite songs), I believed those words but was having a hard time feeling them.

The week prior had been extremely difficult. My nine-month-old son was still having rogue electrical charges pulsing through his brain, and the doctor was concerned. After the most recent test, which had happened earlier that week, the doctor had said, "It's not discouraging, but it's not encouraging." As you can imagine, to my mommy heart, "not encouraging" was the *exact same thing* as "discouraging."

We faced a second challenge that same week: Josiah had outgrown his infant car seat, and we found ourselves needing to trade in one of our vehicles to accommodate a larger seat. On top of that, our first medical bills had arrived. It felt as if problems were ganging up on us.

All of these worries ran through my head as I tried to worship. I believed God was good. He had provided me with a godly husband after many years of waiting, and 15 months later He'd given us Josiah. I knew God loved my son and had a plan for him, but I still grappled with deep discouragement in the midst of uncertainty.

Before Josiah got sick, Kevin and I had often gone out to dinner after church to our favorite Italian place. We would talk about what God had spoken to us during the service and how we might respond as a family. That night we almost didn't go. We knew we didn't have the money. But we finally decided to go and share a pizza to keep the cost low. We had a refreshing conversation as we ate our pizza and salad with Josiah sleeping in his infant carrier beside us.

At the end of the meal, the server came to our table and said, "Someone has paid for your meal. They want to thank you for everything you're doing in the children's ministry." My eyes welled up, overwhelmed by God's goodness through this anonymous gift. The unexpected gift communicated God's love for us in a tangible way, which was just what my heart needed.

I love Jesus' words in Matthew 6:25-27:

> Therefore I tell you, do not worry about your life, what you will eat or drink; or about your body, what you will wear. Is not life more than food, and the body more than clothes? Look at the birds of the air; they do not sow or reap or store away in barns, and yet your heavenly Father feeds them. Are you not much more valuable than they? Can any one of you by worrying add a single hour to your life?

That season was fraught with potential worries. Would my baby recover and continue to develop? Would we be able to pay the mounting medical bills? Would we find a new vehicle that would work for our family? And underlying every worry was one big worry: *Will everything turn out okay?*

But God was writing a story. And as we continued to praise Him and cling to His love and promises, He stepped in to remind us that He saw what was happening and would provide. In a very hard season, I learned to know God in a new, deeper way. As I saw Him care for us in every little detail, and through people I never would have expected, I became more convinced than ever that the suffering and tragedy we had experienced was intentional, and it was for God's glory and our good.

Maybe you have worries today. Maybe you're wondering if

everything is going to turn out okay. I'm here to tell you it will. That doesn't mean the end result will be what you expected or even hoped for. But that's okay. God sees you. He holds you. And He loves you. Oh, how He loves you.

Lord, thank You for loving me. I am amazed by the specific ways in which You care for me and my family. Help me rest in Your love and care when I am worried. Remind me that You are good and have a plan even when I suffer. I love You, Lord! Amen.

Doing Hard Things

—— *Gretta* ——

Sitting in an airplane with a baby on my lap is not among my top ten favorite activities. Don't get me wrong, I love a baby on my lap, but when that baby has to stay put for five hours while we fly across the country…that's just asking for trouble. Titus was three and a half months old when I found myself sitting on a plane, feeling the wetness of trouble protruding from his diaper 30,000 feet in the air. It's not a feeling a mom ever enjoys, but knowing you're going to need to walk the length of the plane and enter the tiniest change station known to mankind to take care of the problem really doesn't invoke excitement at all. But change his diaper I must.

Leaving Kaia with Jay, I grabbed the diaper bag and the baby and made my way to the exceptionally small lavatory at the back of the plane. Courage in hand, I headed in. I immediately felt the sticky and slightly wet floor (eww!) beneath my feet, but tried not to think of it beyond remembering to let nothing else touch said floor. Keeping a firm grasp on Titus, I lowered the change table so it rested on the min-iature counter to the right and the bracket on the left wall hovering about a foot above the toilet. I then laid Titus on paper towels on top of the table, and realizing there was no clean surface to rest the diaper bag, I hung it diagonally across my body. Armed with enough wipes to cover a small country, I got to work. His young bodily efforts required me to strip Titus down to nakedness. Through his protests, he eventually got cleaned up, but I had to laugh—somewhat through exasperation and somewhat through the sheer craziness of the task. With no room to move, I bumped into the walls several times, banging and knocking all round. And as I changed his clothes and freshened him up, I was amazed how difficult this task was. It's no small feat changing a poop-laden baby in an airplane bathroom, but it's necessary. It's not glamorous—the opposite in fact—but it must be done.

Hard work is just that. It's hard. But it must be done to thrive. Staying the course when it gets difficult is vital. First Corinthians 15:58 says, "Therefore, my dear brothers and sisters, stand firm. Let nothing move you. Always give yourselves fully to the work of the Lord, because you know that your labor in the Lord is not in vain."

There is constantly work to be done. Of course there's the practical work of changing the diapers and feeding the children. But then there's the unseen, really hard work of forgiveness, of building Christlike character. The work of humility and standing firm to resist sin. The work of being an image bearer of the one true God. This is hard work. Paul, the author here, said, "Let nothing move you." He wouldn't say that unless there were forces and circumstances trying to change your focus and purpose. No, he said to stay the course of the work of the Lord. It's God's job to change hearts, to build character, and to refine His people to be more like Him.

But we have a part too. And that's to be immovable and push through the hard things. The promise we are given is that all our efforts are not for us. Rather, they are for the Lord's glory, His purpose, and the rewards of heaven. Now, this may sound heavy, but really it's glorious. There is great reward when we do the hard things God has called us to. And you know, He promises His presence, power, and peace while we persevere. Pushing through to complete the task of changing filthy Titus in the plane bathroom wasn't easy, but we all benefited. Happy baby and odor-free air. The rewards of persevering through hard work in your life bring glory to God and peace to all those who benefit from God's work in your life.

So what hard work sits before you? He who called you is faithful and will equip you to the task. So walk in strength and dignity as you push ahead and let nothing move you.

———————

God, give me strength to push through and do the difficult things You've called me to do. Help me not get distracted or discouraged and to stand firm as I follow Your lead in my life. Amen.

Basking in the Path of Totality

———— Suzanne ————

Raising a three-year-old is an exercise in futility. Here are a few statements that regularly cross my lips:

"Don't drink the bath water."

"Don't play in the mud in your good shoes."

"Don't paint the blue hair gel all over your eyebrows."

Don't. Don't. Don't.

Before I was a parent, I always heard people talk about the "Terrible Twos," but I'm here to tell you the threes are worse. In my experience, this seems to be the age when the child's peak craving for independence coincides with her greatest lack of maturity and judgment. This is a dangerous combination that can produce some truly terrible results.

Our daughter Amelia turned three the summer of the total solar eclipse in the United States. For that once-in-a-lifetime event, people booked hotel rooms and campsites months in advance to be in the "Path of Totality," where the moon would completely cover the sun for a few minutes. I told Kevin we could have saved them time and money and just told them to come to our house: My three-year-old *was* the "Path of Totality."

The total destruction, noise, and chaos that one little three-year-old body can create in a short amount of time is almost unfathomable—getting into my makeup and giving herself a "makeover," decorating a wooden chair with dozens of tiny stickers, bursting a box of cereal all over the floor, pulling *every* sock (and pair of underwear) out of the sock drawer, filling the potty with yards of toilet tissue, and leaving moldy, half-eaten remnants of string cheese under the bed. Most days I feel as if Pandora's box has been opened and that stuff is never, ever going back in.

For a person with some control issues, the utter lack of power over such a spirited (and industrious!) little person can be overwhelming, to say the least. These are the parenting moments where I feel like pulling out my hair. And they come at me over and over again, like snowflakes on a car windshield (or bugs if you live in the South).

James 1:2-4 says,

> Consider it pure joy, my brothers and sisters, whenever you face trials of many kinds, because you know that the testing of your faith produces perseverance. Let perseverance finish its work so that you may be mature and complete, not lacking anything.

It may be a touch overdramatic to call these mishaps "trials." However, when I usher my daughter back to her bedroom for the fifth time of the night or help her pick up the playroom, only to have it look like a tornado struck five minutes later, it certainly *feels* like a trial. That said, do you hear what James is saying here? Big or small, these "trials of many kinds" are creating something beautiful in me. These little, daily tests are adding up to maturity and completeness...you could even say *totality.*

I'm thinking maybe those solar eclipse enthusiasts who wanted to bask in the awesomeness of the "Path of Totality" were on to something. There is excitement to be had in being in the moment with my wildly creative, energetic, and resourceful daughter! There is joy in being overwhelmed by this massive life force in a tiny body. It's beautiful. It's distinct. And it will be over before I know it.

Consider it pure joy, Mama. The messes and misadventures. The disasters and discoveries. The calamities and creativity. One day you will say, "I was there. I witnessed it firsthand. And it was beautiful!" Resistance may be futile, but you will live to tell about it. And you will come out the other side a more complete person.

———————

Lord, thank You for the gift of my child. I am amazed at Your handiwork! Help me appreciate the way You have wired my child and the details that make her unique. Through the trials and challenges of parenting, I pray that You would mature me and make me more complete. Help me to be in the moment with my child and give me joy in the memories we are making. Amen.

Thanksgiving Failure

—— *Gretta* ——

Thanksgiving morning came with welcomed excitement as we headed to the airport to spend five days in Edmonton, Alberta, with Jay's parents. I was roughly seven months pregnant with Koen, Kaia was two and a half, and wee Titus had just passed his first birthday. We hadn't seen Nana and Papa for ten months, and since the babies had grown rapidly since our last visit, I was excited for them to show off their new tricks for the grandparents.

The night before I had gone through all the usual last-minute details—flight times, check. Diapers and wipes, check. Snacks for the plane, check. We were ready. So when my dad dropped us off at the airport, we said good-bye and stood in line to check our bags and pick up our boarding passes. We stepped up to the ticketing agent with all our gear, she took our information, our passports, and Titus's birth certificate, and then promptly informed us she couldn't give 13-month-old Titus a boarding pass. "He needs a passport to fly to Canada," she said. I stared at her in disbelief. "But I read on all the information that a lap child can fly on a birth certificate when accompanied by a parent," came my tearful reply. She told us that was true for domestic flights and that actually Titus could fly to Canada on the birth certificate, but since he would need a passport to get back to the United States, she could not give him a boarding pass.

We moved to the side in shock to make our next decision. As you can imagine, I was a wreck. Seven months pregnant, two small children, an upset husband, a busy airport filled with people all trying to make it home for Thanksgiving...I was overwhelmed. I had no idea how to fix this, but one thing was certain—Titus would not be going to see Nana and Papa.

Instead, we left Titus behind with my parents and journeyed just the three of us to Canada. I never questioned whether Titus was in capable hands with my parents, but I can tell you, I felt like the biggest failure all weekend for leaving him behind. Knowing it was my mistake that prevented Jay's parents from seeing their grandson was gut-wrenching. They never said anything about it. Maybe Jay had warned them. Or maybe my sobbing when I saw them as I got off the plane and my perpetual "I'm so sorry" said through tears kept them quiet. Regardless, I knew this was not how it was supposed to be.

This story is still painful for me. When we travel as a family, especially when we are flying—and doubly when we are flying internationally—I get a bit of anxiety. It's in those moments I have to remember Psalm 46:1,5: "God is our refuge and strength, an ever-present help in trouble...God is within her, she will not fall; God will help her at break of day." Satan wants to remind me of my failure and beat me down with it. But God wants me to know He is my strength and my help. There is no need to be crushed by my failures.

I'm not the only one who has ever failed. I'm reminded of Peter's many experiences and failures with Jesus. He got to walk on water, but he focused on the storm and began to sink. He joined Jesus on the Mount of Olives while Jesus was praying in His darkest hour, but not only did he fall asleep while he was supposed to be supporting, once he woke up, in his zeal he cut off a soldier's ear and he was rebuked for it. He claimed to love Jesus and said he would follow Him forever, then denied Him three times while Jesus was on trial for His life. If ever there was a person who failed, it was Peter. He had every reason to look at all his mistakes and give up. But the most encouraging thing to me is that he didn't.

When he sank, he called for help. When he cut off the ear, he learned Jesus had a bigger plan. When he denied knowing Jesus, he asked for forgiveness and then never did it again. And in the end, God used Peter mightily to start His church and spread the gospel.

Struggles in life are inevitable. Failure will happen. But the wise woman realizes that God's refuge and strength, His help in times of trouble will be what she needs in order to not fear. To move on. To overcome. That's what Psalm 46:2 says: "Therefore we will not fear."

Nope. We put on our big-girl panties and get up again. And again. It's not easy to do. But with God's help we can. Where have you failed and need to move forward in victory? What are you punishing yourself for that you need to let go of and claim God's strength and help in? Do it! Walk forward without fear of failing. God is within you. You will not fall!

Lord, oh how I need Your strength when I feel like I've desperately failed and just can't move on! Help me claim these promises in my life and not fear what may come, but move ahead in boldness and victory, knowing You are my help when I face trouble. Amen.

21

Flawed and Loving It

—— *Suzanne* ——

I'm a perfectionist. I'll admit it. The thing is, when I had kids, perfection went so far out the window it landed in the next county. Thus began an embroiled inner struggle that continues to this day: When I can't do things perfectly, I feel like a failure. Maybe you've been there.

I'm not saying I was ever actually perfect. My house was often messy before I had kids to blame (they just took it to a whole new level). And I didn't always live my Christian life seamlessly or treat others in a loving way. In fact, I think I've always been pretty aware of my flaws.

But being a mom threw all of these other *things* into the mix: meal planning, cooking, budgeting, birthday parties, shopping, sports, activities, doctor appointments, school. Caring for the physical, emotional, and spiritual needs of my children presented so many opportunities to fail—so many chances to be imperfect.

A lie of our culture is that perfect is achievable or even normal. And so I put pressure on myself to keep the house clean, *while also* dishing up healthy, kid-pleasing meals, *while also* maintaining a perfect figure, *while also* working, *while also* providing my child with a plethora of experiences and social opportunities, *while also*…and the list goes on. "While also" gets exhausting. And the more I pile on and try to achieve, the more I feel like I'm not doing anything well. And soon my whole identity is wrapped up in what I'm failing at.

This is not God's way. Yes, this is a demanding time of life. Yes, I often feel like I'm not measuring up (mom guilt, anyone?). Yes, I fail to do things perfectly, or even well, every…single…day. (*Sheesh!* Even reading Proverbs 31 can make me feel inadequate.) But God does not want me to live in that place.

Paul the apostle faced a low time in his ministry. He described it as a thorn in his flesh—an aggravation sent to keep him from becoming conceited. Now, I'm not saying being a mom is a thorn in my flesh, but it sure keeps me from being conceited. It's a constant, everyday reminder of my weakness.

How did Paul handle the thorn? He ultimately accepted that his weakness was the very thing God was using to show His power. Listen to what he says in 2 Corinthians 12:10: "That is why, for Christ's sake, I delight in weaknesses, in insults, in hardships, in persecutions, in difficulties. For when I am weak, then I am strong."

What an amazing paradox. When I feel at my worst, God shows His best. His greatest work takes place in the midst of imperfection. So I can remove that self-imposed need to be perfect and rest in His sufficient grace. I don't have to be perfect at everything, and neither do you. Instead, we can faithfully do our best and trust God to use us in spite of our weaknesses.

Perfection may still nip at my heels sometimes, but when I feel like I'm not cutting it, all I have to do is remember *I don't have to.* I am strongest when I am weak. And so are you.

———

Lord, I am so imperfect. Thank You for knowing all of the areas where I am weak and loving me in spite of my failures. I pray that I would lean into You in my weakness so that You look good and receive all of the glory. I invite You to work Your mighty power and strength in me today. Amen.

22

The Lost Child

—— *Gretta* ——

I tend to be a pretty laid-back person, but I had an experience that
sent me into a full-on panic. I was attending a women's home
Bible study. It was ideal because we brought our children, and
while Bible study met upstairs in the cozy living room, we women
rotated taking care of the kids in an incredible basement playroom. The
setup was perfect. It quickly became the highlight of my week. Sweet
fellowship and time in the Word fed my soul. It often got a bit chaotic when our meetings ended: women finishing conversation, 15 or
so babies and toddlers released back into the care of their mamas, people leaving to continue their day.

One afternoon, as I gathered my things and prepared to leave, I
had baby Titus in my arms, but where was Kaia? I calmly checked the
rooms, the basement, and the bathrooms. And then I checked again.
She was nowhere. A couple friends noticed my wide eyes darting to and
fro, and I'm pretty sure they could hear the loud thumping of my heart
protruding from my chest. In no time, all the mamas with free hands
were looking for my two-year-old. I passed Titus off to a friend so I
could look more quickly and thoroughly around the house. I looked
everywhere I hadn't looked before—under beds, in closets, behind the
couch. She had vanished. So we took the search outside and looked

in the play area, around the cars, and all around the house. But again, no Kaia.

The home was out in the country with a long driveway and a pasture separating the road from the house. I have no idea how long we searched—it certainly felt like an eternity—but the longer we looked, the more my internal panic grew. *How could she be gone for this long? There are 15 women here—why has nobody seen her? Where in the world is she?!*

Just as I was about to really start panicking, I saw my friend walking toward me with Kaia in her arms. I immediately ran to her and held Kaia. Boy, did the tears flow then. And actually, come to think of it, I was closer to sobbing. Kaia was safe. She was in my arms. She had somehow slipped out of the door when no one was looking because she wanted to see the horsey in the pasture.

There are few things that send me into a panic. Losing my two-year-old definitely falls into that category. But you know something that never crossed my mind? I never thought, *Oh, you know, Gretta, you have Titus and you're pregnant with another child. It's okay if you never find Kaia.* That would be absolutely absurd! Not a chance. She's my child, and I will do whatever it takes to get her back.

God feels the same way about His kids. Jesus told the story of a shepherd with 100 sheep and one had gone missing. The shepherd left the 99 remaining sheep to go look for the one missing. We don't know how long the shepherd looked, but we know he didn't stop until he found the lost sheep. Where did the sheep go? Did she wander down the hill looking for better grass? Did she get offended by the other sheep around her and decide she needed some personal space? The story doesn't tell us because that's not the important part. The part we're supposed to see is that the shepherd cared so much about the lost sheep he searched until he found her again.

Jesus was very clear in His message: The Shepherd loves His sheep. "And when he finds it, he joyfully puts it on his shoulders and goes home. Then he calls his friends and neighbors together and says, 'Rejoice with me; I have found my lost sheep.' I tell you that in the same way there will be more rejoicing in heaven over one sinner who repents than over ninety-nine righteous persons who do not need to repent" (Luke 15:5-7).

There are many ways we stray from God's perfect design for our lives. Sometimes it's intentional—"I want to do what I want to do and nobody, not even God, is going to stop me." But often we wander without realizing. We fall into patterns of behavior or thinking that are far from God's best. We turn into the complaining, irritable mama. Or the gossiping friend. Or maybe even the selfish spouse. Regardless, it happens, and I'm here to tell you, your Shepherd will not stop pursuing you. He will find your heart and rejoice like crazy when you return to Him.

So where are you today? Do you hear Him calling? Your Shepherd is looking to joyfully carry you back home.

God, it's amazing to me how quickly I wander, thinking I can find something better. Thank You for the promise that You will always look for me. You never give up the search. Help me stay close to You, no matter how green the grass looks in the next pasture. Thank You for being such a Good Shepherd. Amen.

23

Special Day

—— *Suzanne* ——

The summer before he went into kindergarten, Josiah qualified for extended school year, where he would attend five additional weeks of school. For the first time, we opted for him to take the bus to and from school. The first day, as we waited in front of our house for the bus to arrive, Josiah was bursting with excitement. "This is a special day!" he proclaimed over and over.

When the yellow bus pulled into our neighborhood, Josiah jumped up and down. "It's the bus! The bus is here!" he yelled.

I smiled at his enthusiasm and snapped pictures of him getting on the bus and waving good-bye. While I expected his excitement on the first day, I was surprised to see that his enthusiasm never waned for the entire summer. Each day he greeted the bus with the same level of excitement and joy. Whether it was Monday or Thursday, he would proclaim, "This is a special day!" To him, the simple joy of riding the bus made the day top-notch.

His sentiments echo what the psalmist said in Psalm 118:24: "This is the day that the Lord has made; let us rejoice and be glad in it" (ESV). I am not a morning person, so I rarely greet the morning the way my son does. But he's right: Today *is* a special day! Why? Because God has made it. And my response should be to rejoice and be glad in it.

Doing that is not always easy. When I'm running low on sleep and overwhelmed by my to-do list, rejoicing isn't my normal response. I can so easily focus on the burdens and worries of the day and miss the beauty that surrounds me.

My little boy has been a good example to me of how I need to view my days. Each day I wake up and have the opportunity to serve and love my husband and babies is a "special day." The sun rising and fresh air to breathe is a gift from God. I simply have to have the right attitude. Anticipating all that God will do in and through me in the day He has crafted should inspire gladness.

Years have passed since Josiah's first bus ride, but he still loves busses. Last year we made him a bus costume out of a cardboard box and yellow paint. One of his favorite things to do is put on his costume and pretend he's picking up kids and driving them to school.

Each morning he watches from our front window for the bus to arrive. When he sees it drive up, he still yells out, "The bus is here! The bus is here!" with the exact same excitement he had on that first day.

I want to begin my days with that same joy. And I can because God has made today and I get to be part of it! That makes every day a special day.

———

Lord, thank You for creating each new day and inviting me to be a part of it. I praise You for each sweet moment with my family and each breath. Help me recognize that my days come from You and take joy in them. You are a good God. Give me childlike excitement to greet each beautiful day You give me. Amen.

24

Joining the Work

—— *Gretta* ——

One of my favorite smells in the world is freshly cut grass on a warm summer day. At two years old, our daughter seemed to think so as well. Our home had a perfectly sized small fenced backyard that only took 20 minutes to mow with our push mower. Every week Jay would go out to cut the lawn, and every week, when she heard the motor start up, Kaia ran to her daddy's side and held his hand while he mowed. Back and forth across the yard they walked, making stripes in the grass and filling the air with the sweet aroma I love so much. In the beginning Kaia walked just holding his hand, but as she grew, she was able to eventually hold the handle along with him. But she always, and I mean always, insisted on mowing with her daddy.

Whenever they finished the yard, it was Kaia who would run to me and excitedly say, "Mama, I mowed!" "Yes, sweetheart, you did," I'd reply. "You did great!" As her mother, I of course knew it wasn't Kaia who mowed the lawn, but I recognized that she was working and was proud of the job she had done. I encouraged her to keep working hard and enjoying being with her daddy. The time they spent every week mowing was delightful. Kaia joined the work of her father. It wasn't a burden. It was fun (though occasionally she would grunt as they turned the mower). Kaia loved mowing, and she really did think she was the one doing all the work. But let's face it, she was only joining in with the one who had the resources, the strength, and the design for what was to be done.

Work is important. We were created with the need to work and have purpose. Even before sin entered the world, Adam and Eve were given jobs. But somewhere along the way we have come to believe that the things we do define us. We believe that it's our duty to hold everything together. And while, yes, we have responsibilities, it's not in our power or our burden to change people and circumstances. That's our Father's job. He never asks us to do the work on our own or to carry the burden of responsibility.

Instead, we actually get to take the role of Kaia mowing the lawn. We get to join God at work. He is the one with the strength, resources, and design. The apostle Paul understood this when he said in 1 Corinthians 3:9, "We are co-workers in God's service." And Psalm 127:1 says, "Unless the LORD builds the house, the builders labor in vain. Unless the LORD watches over the city, the guards stand watch in vain." You see, God is actually the one doing all the work. He's the architect and the protector; we join in.

How exactly do we join in what God is doing? When we model kindness and compassion instead of anger and bitterness, we show a bit of Jesus. When we offer a listening ear to a friend really struggling with life, we partner with God as He ministers to her soul. When we teach our children about Jesus, we join God in raising the next generation of Christ followers. Where we get it wrong sometimes is when we think the responsibility of changing hearts is ours. But that's God's job. God is the one actually pushing the lawn mower and doing the work, but He longs for and delights in us partnering with Him.

This means it's not all on your shoulders to make sure everything happens. It's not solely your responsibility to make sure your kids love Jesus or that your relationship with your in-laws is without conflict. God is the one who builds the house. He is in charge, and we hold His hand while He pushes the mower. That should alleviate some of the pressure. Your responsibility is to remain faithful in obedience to Him, but He does the real work.

––––––––––––

God, thank You for holding everything together. Help me change my thinking to understanding that You are in control and it's not my job to do all the work. Thank You for instead allowing me to join You and not be burdened about the results of the work. Amen.

25

Invited and Seen

—— *Suzanne* ——

Not long ago I got bummed out when my five-year-old wasn't invited to a birthday party. It seems kind of silly now. She was completely unaware of the fact, so it didn't cause her any emotional distress. And the birthday girl was a fringe acquaintance, so it wasn't an intentional slight. But viewing the pictures online and seeing a lot of other kids we knew, I felt left out and a little hurt for my daughter. *Why wasn't she invited?*

As moms we worry about our kids making social connections and fitting in. But I think my reaction went deeper than that. Sadie had not a care in the world and has plenty of friends; *I* was the one feeling excluded. I wish I could say this was the first time I allowed my own insecurities to make me miserable, but I can't. It's happened before. And no doubt it will happen again.

Rejection is real, and it stings. In the Old Testament, we read about a mama who was feeling some serious rejection. The beginning of the story reads like a soap opera. Hagar was Sarai's slave. When Sarai couldn't get pregnant, she encouraged Abram to marry Hagar and sleep with her to bring about the child God had promised.

Abram did, and Hagar became pregnant. Predictably, all hades broke loose. Hagar despised Sarai. Sarai mistreated Hagar. Finally, desperate and miserable, Hagar fled to the desert and stopped by a spring. She must have felt very alone, but she wasn't.

The Lord came to her and assured her that He would make her descendants great in number. He told her that she was carrying a son who would be a mighty man, and his name was Ishmael. The Lord instructed her to return to Abram and Sarai, which she eventually did.

But listen to Hagar's response to this supernatural encounter: "She gave this name to the LORD who spoke to her: 'You are the God who sees me,' for she said, 'I have now seen the One who sees me'" (Genesis 16:13).

Hagar was the first to call God *El Roi*, the God who sees. In every rejection, real or imagined, God sees me. When I'm feeling like no one cares, He does. When I feel excluded, He extends an open invitation.

Are you feeling rejected today, Mama? Are you feeling left out or uninvited? We all experience situations where we feel overlooked or like nobody cares. But those feelings couldn't be further from the truth. Our loving heavenly Father sees us and cares deeply about our feelings.

Not only that, but Jesus knows what rejection feels like. Isaiah 53:3 says, "He was despised and rejected by mankind, a man of suffering, and familiar with pain. Like one from whom people hide their faces he was despised, and we held him in low esteem." Have you ever really thought about the fact that our Savior, the humble One we pattern our lives after, was never one of the "cool kids"? Although many were drawn to Him because of His love, He faced ultimate rejection when He died a humiliating death on the cross.

While my daughter was blissfully unaware of missing this party, a day will come where she won't be invited and she *will* understand. How will I help her wade through the emotions of rejection then? The same way I'm dealing with them now, by helping her look to Jesus, the One who sees her disappointment and understands exactly how she feels.

––––––––

Lord, sometimes I allow trivial things to make me feel excluded or less than. Other times I feel the sting of true rejection. Thank You for being the God who sees and meets me in my pain. Thank You for accepting me and offering me an open invitation to a relationship with You. Amen.

26

Soul Food

—— *Gretta* ——

Fissy, Mama, fissy." Titus had been saying it for close to a week in his sweet, almost two-year-old voice. Then the guessing game would start. We were vacationing in Hawaii and had experienced all sorts of wonderful things: snorkeling, hiking, boogie boarding, and great beach time.

"Do you want to see the fish, buddy?"

"No."

"You want to go play in the water?"

"Uh-huh," came his hopeful reply.

I'd walk over and get his swimsuit and he'd start up again.

"No, Mama. Fissy."

"You want to go snorkeling?"

"No."

And this is how the conversation would go for several days. The problem was that he would get increasingly frustrated as the days wore on and the unfruitful dialogue continued. As someone new to the English language, Titus didn't have the best enunciation, nor did he have many other proficient words to draw from. But he wasn't the only frustrated one. Jay and I both felt at a loss in understanding him. We tried all sorts of things, but he just continued.

Then one afternoon, just after his nap, Titus stood, looking up at me in the kitchen, and said, "Fissy, Mama." *Oh, here we go again.* I stared at him for maybe five seconds, tilted my head to the side, and said slowly, "Buddy, are you thirsty?" There was instant relief in his entire body. "Yeah" came the sweet, tender reply. And with that, he drank a huge cup of water.

It was so simple once I figured it out. But it took really putting in the time and effort to decode his language.

Much like Titus, our souls are speaking to us repeatedly. We all have a longing for intimacy, love, peace, rest, relationship. And that soul is crying out to be filled. In fact, our souls speak to us every day and crave satisfaction. You hear it. Though you may not realize it, you hear it. It's your desire to connect with friends. It's your longing to be fully known and understood by your husband. It's that craving for deep rest. So the question is, how do you fill the longing in your soul?

If you're anything like me, when it comes to filling that relational longing, you might turn to social media just to connect with people above the age of five. It's wonderful because it links you to the outside world and you can get a good support system through it. But social media won't fill that longing. Instead, it's like bingeing on potato chips. Though yummy, they are not designed to sustain you.

Or maybe you're looking to your husband to solve all your intimacy needs. The problem here is that your husband has needs of his own and he isn't designed to completely fill you.

Perhaps the desire of your heart for a long time was to be a mother. And here you are. It's good and wonderful and you definitely love this little person more than you thought possible, yet it's still not completely fulfilling. Chances are, you may be hearing your soul cry out "fissy" and think you need to go snorkeling. Close, but not satisfying.

Instead, you need to hear the words of David in Psalm 63: "You, God, are my God, earnestly I seek you; I thirst for you, my whole body longs for you…I will be fully satisfied as with the richest of foods…I cling to you; your right hand upholds me." When we understand that our soul is actually hungry and thirsty for God and we look to Him to feed and nourish it, He actually gives us good food. Psalm 107:9 tells us, "He satisfies the thirsty and fills the hungry with good things." His food is restorative. It's good. There are no potato chips here. No snorkeling. Just good, pure, ice-cold, refreshing water. Satisfying.

How are you feeding your soul? What does it look like to go to God first for that filling? Reading this is a great start. You could write verses on your bathroom mirror with dry-erase pens. You could have worship music playing in the background of your home. You can keep the communication lines of prayer open throughout your day. There are a number of ways to get your filling from God. Then the time with your husband, the checking in with your friends, the other things just become added fillers, and your true nutrition comes from the One who made you. Make today a day of getting soul food from the One who made it.

———

Lord, fill me with You. Give me the good things my soul needs and help me look to You first for satisfaction. Thank You for promising to give me what I need. Give me the courage and strength to not look for "snorkeling" to fill my thirst. Amen.

27

Gentle Shepherd

—— *Suzanne* ——

My husband, Kevin, can always tell when I'm having a really bad mom day. He'll come home from work, and I'll be blasting Christmas music…in May.

"That bad, huh?" he'll quip. He doesn't know the half of it.

I love Christmas music. For years I followed "the rules" and only listened to it during November and December. But since I became a mom and music streaming became a thing, the rules have gone out the window. When I'm sad, overwhelmed, or finding it hard to cope, Christmas music is my antidote.

How about you? How do you cope on hard days? One mom I know retreats to a book after her kids have gone to bed. Another treats herself to a scone and tea each afternoon while her children are napping. Still another plays games on her phone to relieve stress during her limited free time.

Stress is a reality of being a mom. In fact, some studies have found that how parents handle their own stress affects their children more than things they do for their child.* But even when I'm doing my best

---

* "Managing Stress for a Healthy Family," American Psychological Association, accessed May 10, 2018, http://www.apa.org/helpcenter/managing-stress.aspx.

to minimize stress, a hectic situation can strike at any moment. I have had many days where I texted Kevin that everything was great at 3:30 p.m. (and it was), but by the time he arrived home from work, I was a sniveling basket case with the kids running amok around me. Maybe you've been there. No, just me?

God understands the stress that comes with being a mom. In fact, in Isaiah 40:11, we hear about His special treatment for mothers: "He tends his flock like a shepherd: He gathers the lambs in his arms and carries them close to his heart; he gently leads those that have young."

These years of having a young family are equal parts excitement and strain. Not only are you attending to your own needs, you are managing the needs (and demands) of multiple others. I recently took a birthday trip with a girlfriend. It was the first time I had flown alone since having children. I tried to describe to her how when I'm in the airport with children my mind is constantly filled to the brim with concerns and logistical details to the point that I scarcely notice all that is going on around me. My mommy brain constantly has "browser tabs" open for each of my children.

So it's comforting to know God cares about our "lambs" and holds them close to His heart. Not only that, He notices our special role as mothers caring for our young. He understands when we are preoccupied with our children or worried about them. But in the midst of it, He is an unfailingly Good Shepherd to all of us.

Jesus said, "I am the good shepherd; I know my sheep and my sheep know me—just as the Father knows me and I know the Father—and I lay down my life for the sheep" (John 10:14-15). He knows you, Mama. He understands the path you're walking. And He is committed to leading you with gentleness. He gave His life for you; why would He not care for your lambs?

When I'm having a "Christmas music" day, no matter the time of year, I can remember I walk with a Good Shepherd who understands and guides me every step of the way. Be gentle with yourself today, Mama. Your Good Shepherd is with you.

Lord, thank You for loving my children and having a special place in Your heart for me as their mother. On stressful days help me know that You are near. Hold me close and help me trust You as the Good Shepherd and follow You on sweet days and hard ones. Amen.

28

Life-Giving Groups

—— *Gretta* ——

J ay and I had been married just under a year when we joined our first life group. Our church worked hard to get everyone connected with a smaller group of people for the purpose of having other Christians who know you and your story, and can encourage your growth as a believer. For three years we tried out different groups, hoping to find a good fit. Each group provided us with fellowship, biblical teaching, and encouragement, but it wasn't until the fourth year before we found a group that truly fed our souls.

Our group consisted of five couples, four of whom had small children at home and one couple with grown kids who led us. Kaia was two, Titus nearly one, and I was pregnant with Koen so we got a babysitter every week. Our group met three weeks in a row when we worked our way through a parenting video or a marriage book and then the fourth week we shared a meal together. As we met week after week, we slowly got to know each other better, opened up more, and got real. So real, in fact, I even remember the women sitting around the table one night talking about our placentas as though it were a normal dinnertime topic! No one was squirmy or batted an eye as we compared stories.

I don't remember the videos we watched or what books we read together, but I do remember sharing our birth stories. I remember talking about the frequency of our babies' poo. We discussed the complexities of keeping a marriage healthy when time alone and awake rarely occurred. One evening as we were discussing a few of the demands on us wives at home, our leader spoke about what he was like as a young husband. He opened up about his own shortcomings as a clueless new father, and in doing so, he gave us space to be weak together. This was a place and a time we were all committed to and where we knew we were like-minded, loved, accepted, and encouraged. We cried together, laughed together, and shared our lives.

Jay and I only stayed one year with that group because we moved to Canada shortly after Koen was born, but we still occasionally talk about that life group and the profound impact it had on us as young parents. It wasn't magical; it was just Hebrews 10:24-25 in action, which says, "Let us…not [give] up meeting together, as some are in the habit of doing, but [encourage] one another—and all the more as you see the Day approaching."

Could we have made it in those days as newlyweds and then as a young budding family without our life group? Sure we could have. But by meeting together regularly and sharing our lives, we were able to learn from others, lean on others, and share our own journey and struggles with them. In a way, we were able to do more thriving than surviving because of that group. We had support. We had encouragement. We didn't feel alone in the journey.

Do you need some support right now? Is your circle of friends encouraging you to grow as a mom, a friend, a wife, and a child of God? I encourage you to find a group of other Christians to join in your journey. You may think, like I did at times, that getting together with others on a weekly basis might feel like one more thing to add to your already overwhelmed life. But let me assure you, if you are meeting with the right people who build you up, support you, and offer a safe place to be weak, you will not only look forward to gathering together, you will feel more alive and able to keep pressing forward in what God has placed before you. It will be life-giving!

—————

Lord, You have given us one another to encourage and support each other. Thank You for not creating us to do life alone. Give me the courage to step out and join or create a group and not give up meeting together so we can thrive in this journey. Amen.

29

Joy for the Asking

—— *Suzanne* ——

One Sunday afternoon I decided to take my oldest son to the grocery store, which was kind of a big deal. Due to his developmental issues, Josiah generally struggles on focusing and self-regulating in exciting places like stores, so I avoid taking him. But this particular afternoon I had a short list, so I decided to brave it.

It had been several months since we'd attempted it by ourselves, so I laid out the rules while we were still in the car:

1. Stay by the shopping cart.

2. Don't run away from Mommy.

3. When Mommy calls, come right back.

I noticed right away when we got into the store that he was having an easier time abiding by our rules than he had in the past. I smiled as he helped me push the cart and asked if we could get a bag of Granny Smith apples (his favorite). I tossed the bag into the cart, no questions asked.

In the cereal aisle, he requested marshmallow cereal. Although I try to keep sugary snacks out of the house, the bright-red box of cereal went into the cart. A box of graham crackers, a bag of Skittles, and a six-pack of his favorite soda later, I realized I'd been whipped—by a tow-headed seven-year-old with a toothless grin.

The experience was emotional for me as I thought back to Josiah's rocky journey of growing up that began with a seizure disorder as an infant. As a four-year-old, he had barely noticed there were groceries in the store, being obsessed instead with the fans, lights, and motion-detecting doors. And in kindergarten he still couldn't make simple requests at home or school for what he wanted.

So watching him confidently stroll through the store, asking me for his favorite treats, felt like nothing short of a miracle. Hearing him ask me for things filled my mama heart with joy! You better believe I was going to reward him for asking.

Many of you mamas probably wish your children would *stop* asking for things at the store, but I believe God gave me this unique experience with my son to remind me of His Father heart for me.

Psalm 37:4 reveals God's beautiful intentions toward us: "Take delight in the Lord, and he will give you the desires of your heart." He cares about the desires of your heart, Mama. Throughout Scripture, He invites us over and over again to *ask*. Listen to what Jesus told His disciples in John 15:7: "If you remain in me and my words remain in you, ask whatever you wish, and it will be done for you."

As I sat in the car, Josiah munching contentedly on one of his treats in the back seat, I thought about how God must love to hear us ask. Just as I took joy in hearing my son ask me to provide for the desires of his heart, God must love to hear me ask Him for the things I want and need.

So many times I exhaust other resources before I think to ask Him. And yet He is always there—a prayer away—just waiting for me to ask. Mama, next time you're tempted to squelch a desire or dream, or think a request is too much to ask for, ask anyway! Your heavenly Father wants to hear from you. He loves to give His children good gifts. He might even surprise you with the extravagance of His generosity.

Lord, thank You for loving me and inviting me to ask You for the things I need and want. I confess that sometimes I simply forget to ask. Today I lay my needs and desires at Your feet. I trust You, Father. Thank You for hearing my requests and giving me good gifts. Help me have a childlike faith. Amen.

30

Easter Basket Goodness

Gretta

Kaia was dressed in a cute springtime outfit and held on to her precious pink basket as she stood in line along with a hundred other little toddlers her age. Our town had taken over the community park for a citywide Easter egg hunt. Hundreds of parents were there with kids of all ages waiting for their age category to have a turn finding eggs. Sectioned off by flagging tape, each age category had a big square area filled with brightly colored eggs. And by filled, I mean there were so many eggs that you could see more colors on the ground than grass. This wasn't so much of a "hunt" as a walk-and-pick-up-the-egg-in-front-of-you type of event.

So we waited for our turn. As soon as they said, "Go," Kaia crossed the line with the other children and began picking up eggs. One by one she added them to her basket, delighting each time her little two-year-old self found another treasure. In a matter of about 30 seconds, the two-year-old category had cleaned up their square, leaving only grass behind. It went insanely fast. Kaia had so much fun, and we could tell she wasn't done "finding" eggs, so when she wasn't looking, Jay grabbed an egg from her basket and tossed it directly in her path. Then, with joy, she exclaimed, "Ooh, another one!" and immediately put it in her basket. This never-ending egg game continued for quite some time. Kaia didn't tire from finding each egg, and we certainly enjoyed giving more and more to our daughter.

Her discovery and delight in finding each egg reminded me of God's mercy and steadfast love. God's love never ends, and His mercy and compassion can't stop either. It's just who He is. Lamentations 3:22-23 are a fantastic reminder of His unyielding character: "Because of the LORD's great love we are not consumed, for his compassions never fail. They are new every morning; great is your faithfulness."

Every morning there's a new Easter egg of mercy. Did you notice how those verses lay out? It is *because* of God's immense love for us that we are not consumed by our sin. God is compassionate beyond our ability to use it up, and every morning comes a new, fresh start. This is God's faithful promise.

Do you sometimes feel you've blown it? Perhaps your own frustrations leave you feeling defeated and not the mama you want or ever thought you would be. When the baby just won't. Stop. Crying. Or maybe you lose your temper with your toddler who insists on challenging every word you say with "no." There are a million reasons we can feel defeated and consumed. But let me encourage you, Mama. God is faithful to give you new mercies. More compassion. And He will never stop.

Often those truths were my lifeline. I'd feel so defeated by how I had behaved toward the children or how I had snapped at my husband. There were many times (and to be honest, there still are) when I feel like I am ruining my children or hurting my marriage. But God's promises, faithfulness, and mercy give me the strength and hope to carry on. First John 1:9 tells us that when we mess up, we need to own it and confess it, and that God, in His faithfulness, will forgive us. Then we know we do not need to be consumed by our sin. We walk in the freedom and grace that comes through forgiveness. His compassions are new every morning.

Do you need to notice the Easter egg of God's faithful love and compassion today? Pick it up. It's right there in front of you. I know you mess up, but don't let that defeat you. Confess it, seek forgiveness, and move on in freedom. Tomorrow is a new day with new mercy.

Lord, I really don't like how I've been treating my family lately. I feel like a failure and like I've just really messed up. I don't want to keep behaving like this. Please show me Your new mercies and help me walk forward in that freedom of forgiveness. Amen.

31

Getting Out of
Survival Mode

—— *Suzanne* ——

There's nothing comfortable about being a mom of young children.

When I was single I used to wonder if my mama friends were being a little overly dramatic about the strain of caring for little ones. *My job is hard and stressful too,* I would think. *I feel drained and exhausted at the end of the day.*

Then I became a mom. Now, I am not about to start a debate about which is harder—caring for children or going to work all day (or both!)—but let's just say that I was not prepared for my promotion from office job to "home manager."

My typical day goes something like this: Wake up, feed the kids breakfast, pick up clothes off the floor, unload dishwasher, load dishwasher, sweep floor, start a load of laundry, change diaper, warm baby food, feed baby, wipe baby's face and hands, help toddler go potty, wipe bottom, cut up apple slices for "elevensies" (which comes after first and second breakfast), put dishes in sink, help toddler do craft project that involves glitter, sweep up glitter, fold clothes, wipe table, put baby down for nap, pick up clothes off the floor…and so on into infinity and beyond.

I'd be lying if I said I thrive on these tasks. More like I do them out of a sense of duty. On my best days, like some over-caffeinated Mary Poppins, I try to make these tasks into a game, but many times I find myself just watching that clock inch toward 7:30 so I can put the kids to bed and hit the reset button.

At times I feel ashamed that I feel this way. After all, I'm living my dream. I am *blessed* to have these children. But some days I feel anything but grateful. I feel worn out and overwhelmed and at the end of myself. I worry—no, I'm convinced—that I'm not giving my husband or my children my best. But no matter how hard I try, I can't seem to adjust my thinking to feeling more positive about all I have to do.

Speaking to His disciples, Jesus said, "Come to me, all you who are weary and burdened, and I will give you rest. Take my yoke upon you and learn from me, for I am gentle and humble in heart, and you will find rest for your souls. For my yoke is easy and my burden is light" (Matthew 11:28-30).

That sounds pretty good, doesn't it? In the daily struggle of tackling the to-do list, Jesus says, "Come to me. I will give you rest." *Really, Lord?* I wonder. *How is that possible in the midst of sleep deprivation and seemingly endless demands?*

These years of caring for young children have stretched me to my limits emotionally, mentally, and spiritually more than any other season of my life. And many days I doubt my ability to do it well. But Jesus tells me to *learn from Him.* How would Jesus approach my to-do list? How would He interact with my children? How would He make the most of each opportunity? The amazing truth is that He is with me, by my side, lightening my load and giving me strength as I sweep up the glitter and fold the laundry and wipe little noses.

Being a mom is harder than I thought. But even in this season, Jesus offers me His easy yoke. Somehow He can make heavy loads light. He extends peace and rest to me. What a refreshing truth for wearying days.

———

Lord, sometimes this mom thing is hard and I become
weary. Thank You for inviting me to rest. Thank You

for offering me an easy yoke in a season of so many demands. Help me depend on You as I go about the tasks of my day. Teach me to be gentle and humble of heart as I allow You to lighten my load. Amen.

32

Worms in the Garden

———— *Gretta* ————

I've always encouraged a love for the outdoors in my children, so it was no surprise one warm spring day to find my two oldest digging in garden dirt. They were clothed in nothing but diapers as they collected all the garden worms they could find. We hadn't planted seeds yet, so they had the entire box of rich soil in which to dig and discover. My three-year-old did most of the digging and was covered in brown dirt. The one-and-a-half-year-old was a bit cleaner at first sight, but upon closer inspection I could see the effects of his worm-collecting methods. Since he had no pockets, he would pick up a beloved worm between his thumb and forefinger, then roll the poor thing in his chubby little toddler hand. No worm could survive after that. So though he looked clean-ish, especially compared to his sister, he was perhaps even dirtier than she.

Worm guts are sticky and gooey. And when they get all squished into bits, they travel and get in every nook and cranny. So after taking a few pictures and oohing and aahing over their hard work, the kids were plopped into the bath. It's here where soap and water worked their magic.

Kids get dirty and need bathwater to clean them. A bath is always a special time. With its splashing, bubbles, toys, and games, a bath can take the crabbiest of children and transform them to delightful beings once again. And the hugs that follow when wrapping a soft towel around their sweet-smelling clean bodies is just hard to beat.

But kids aren't the only ones who need cleaning, are they? You and I need this too. We lose our cool. We get impatient. We get tired and snippy. And before you know it, we're covered in dirt with worm guts in every nook and cranny of our lives. So we need to hop into our own bathtub, so to speak.

See, God promises in 1 John 1:9 that "if we confess our sins, he is faithful and just to forgive us our sins and to cleanse us from all unrighteousness" (esv). There is so much packed into that tiny little verse. In this promise God has a job and we have a job. Let me unpack it for just a minute.

God's job…

> He is faithful: Dependable. True. Devoted.
>
> He is just: Fair. Honorable. Nondiscriminatory.
>
> To forgive: Release. Purge. Exonerate. Absolve.
>
> To cleanse: Restore. Clean. Sanitize.
>
> From *all* unrighteousness: Crimes. Wickedness. Offense.

And then there's our job…

> To confess: Acknowledge. Reveal. Declare.
>
> Our sins: All the worm guts. The nasty attitudes. The selfishness. The anger.

Do you see how almost all the work here is God's? All we have to do is confess our sins. Sometimes when we know a verse so well, we stop actually reading the words. Take a moment to change their order to hear it afresh like this: "If we reveal our anger, He is dependable and fair to release us of our anger and to sanitize us from all offense." Do you hear it differently now?

Are you overwhelmed by your selfishness? By your anger? By your constant comparison to other moms?

Isn't it time to hop into God's bathtub and get cleaned up? You may think your dirt is just too much. But I promise you that nothing is too great for the saving work of Jesus. It doesn't matter how many times you've confessed it, He will continually forgive you and give you the strength to grow and move on. And He promises that once He forgives, He never brings it back up. It's like He'll pull the plug and all the sin will go down the drain. Gone forever.

Take little minutes throughout today to confess those things that are making you dirty. And the next time you pull your child out of the tub, smell deeply their clean body and remember God's faithful promise to forgive and cleanse you too.

God, I'm a hot mess. I've got sin I've been holding on to for a while and just need to tell You about it. You promise You're faithful. You promise You are just. And You promise to cleanse me from this sin. So, God, I confess this stuff to You. Thank You for wiping me clean and sanitizing my life. Thank You for not condemning me but for willingly welcoming my confessions over and over again. Thank You that I can always come to You at any time, with anything, and You will forgive me. Amen.

33

Beauty Lost and Found

—— *Suzanne* ——

Ever since I became a mom, beauty has seemed elusive. And while I was no fashion plate before kids, I did have more time to get ready in the morning and was more or less proud of how I looked on a daily basis. Now most days when I get ready, I look in the mirror and feel a lot like Mia Thermopolis in *The Princess Diaries*, who mutters, "And *that's* as good as it's gonna get."

Sometimes when I'm picking up the *same exact toys* off the ground for the umpteenth time, I stare wistfully at the mantle-top photo of Kevin and me on our wedding day. I see the toned arms, thin face, and perfect hair—now replaced by stubborn baby weight, tired eyes, and second (or third) day hair—and I'm convinced I've peaked. *I'm just gonna look like a mom now,* I think. *Might as well accept it.*

Something in me fights that thought, though. If our billion-dollar beauty industry is any indication, most of us long to be beautiful. So it can be demoralizing not to *feel* beautiful for days, months, or years on end. And yet, as moms in a season of putting the needs of others first, this can easily happen. While true beauty isn't dependent on how often I make it to the salon or put on makeup, when I'm pouring myself out for my family and these things fall by the wayside, it's easy to convince myself that my most beautiful days are behind me.

Mama, this kind of thinking is a lie. You are created for beauty. God made you in His image to display His glory and His beauty. Beauty that is so much more than a slim waistline, luminous skin, or silky smooth locks (things that can be hard for any woman to maintain). And while Proverbs tells us that "beauty is fleeting" (31:30), we also see in Scripture that loveliness seems to be part of our very design as women.

One example is found in the Song of Songs, a love poem written by King Solomon about a woman he loves. The book is full of elaborate descriptions of her beauty and reveals her blossoming self-confidence under the adoration of her beloved.

In Song of Songs 4:7, Solomon seems to be shouting her praises from the rooftops: "You are altogether beautiful, my darling; there is no flaw in you."

How much do you and I crave having someone say those words of us? How we long to stand in the confidence that we are beautiful. Many biblical scholars consider Song of Songs to be a picture of how God loves us. At times flaws are all I can see, but God, to whom I am beloved, tells me: "You are beautiful, my darling. I make beautiful things. My beauty shines out of you, even as you wipe sticky little faces, scrub out the potty chair, and do a gazillion loads of laundry."

He's also good at reminding me of that beauty when I'm open to accept it. A few years ago I was in a season where I was often homebound with three young children. One morning I styled my hair and put on makeup in preparation for a rare appointment. As I walked into the playroom, Josiah—five at the time—cupped my face in his hands, looked at me intently, and said, "You look pretty!"

Tears immediately filled my eyes. A man of very few words, Josiah had never said anything like that before. And in that moment I felt more beautiful than I had in a long time. It may be true that "I'm just gonna look like a mom now." But I'm okay with that. Moms are beautiful.

Lord, thank You for creating me and telling me that I am
beautiful. Thank You for making me a mom. Although I

may sometimes feel unattractive or unexceptional during this season of life, I pray I won't focus on my flaws or achieving physical perfection, but that I would allow Your beauty to shine through me in everything I do. Amen.

34

Encourage One Another Daily

—— Gretta ——

The first time I went grocery shopping with all three kids was an adventure, to say the least. My favorite grocery store was 30 minutes away from my home, and with a newborn, a 15-month-old, and an almost 3-year-old, I knew good time management would be key for this trip to succeed. Conveniently situated next to the grocery store was Babies R Us. My genius plan was to stop first at Babies R Us, go to the room at the back for nursing moms, feed Koen while Titus and Kaia played in the small room, and then go next door to get all the food. Everything went well at Babies R Us, and the plan was working perfectly. I knew shopping wouldn't be easy, as we needed a lot of food and, well, I had all these tiny kids. So in the grocery store I wore Koen on my chest, Titus sat in the cart, and Kaia, bless her, sat in the enormous basket.

As we walked up and down the aisles, I bounced Koen and sang softly to the kids. We sang "Jesus Loves Me," "The Itsy Bitsy Spider," and many others. Each item I placed in the cart shrank Kaia's sitting space, but I was determined not to let her out. Cereal, noodles, canned foods, flour, and sugar all surrounded her, and I just continued to sing…"The Wheels on the Bus Go Round and Round"…all through the store.

I have to admit by the time we made it to the frozen food section, all I could see was Kaia's cute little curly hair. We pretended she was taking a silly bath in the food. It wasn't all roses, but we did our best. Aisle by aisle we made it through with minor complaints. When we were in the checkout line, an elderly man stood behind us. He said some of the most encouraging words to me. Apparently he had been following me throughout the store (in a non-creepy sort of way), and my singing and interactions with my kids reminded him of days long gone. He envied that I was in the midst of these demanding, hands-on years. He said these are some of the greatest days in life, and he thanked me for loving my kids.

I was blown away! I was merely trying to figure out a way to survive shopping with all three kids at once. It never occurred to me that anyone would notice or care how I shopped. But this sweet old man touched on something that has been a reminder to me for so many years. Our words matter. Our tone matters.

Ephesians 4:29 tells us, "Don't use foul or abusive language. Let everything you say be good and helpful, so that your words will be an encouragement to those who hear them" (NLT).

This verse has been vital in our home. The NIV uses the phrase "unwholesome talk" instead of "foul or abusive language," which communicates the idea that even tone, along with words, matter. In fact, everything that comes out of our mouths has value. Good or bad. Abusive, foul, unwholesome speech tears others down, belittles, or simply communicates annoyances. But this idea of only allowing the good and helpful words out of your mouth—the words and tone that build others up, that encourage—are actually life-giving.

I found it interesting that when my tone and words were kind and encouraging, my children benefited and even an unknown elderly man was encouraged. In fact, he was so built up that his joy spilled over and back onto me. It was reciprocal. It was mutually edifying.

When was the last time you struggled with this? Yesterday? This morning? Five minutes ago? I understand, Mama. It's hard to keep watch of our tongues. But, dear Mama, it is vitally important to only allow what is good and helpful to come out of your mouth. Your children, your husband, and yes, even the stranger at the grocery store will benefit and be encouraged by it.

———————

Lord, help me control my tongue! Give me an awareness of how my speech and tone can bring encouragement to everyone who hears what I say. Help me today to be helpful and uplifting to my children and everyone I meet. Amen.

35

Just Move

—— *Suzanne* ——

Not long ago I was in love with a particular movie soundtrack and I played the music incessantly for weeks. One day I was washing dishes when both my girls began dancing along to the music in the next room. I smiled at their wild, untrained spins and leaps. I was basically watching my "mommy dreams" for these sweet sisters unfold before my teary eyes.

Then the oldest, Sadie, said, "I have an idea! C'mon." The girls tromped up the stairs to their bedroom and soon returned wearing leotards, tights, and ballet slippers. As I watched them dance as only a three-year-old and a five-year-old can, I marveled at the freedom in their expression. They felt the music, and they simply moved.

I wish I could say that I live my life and calling with a fraction of that exuberant freedom. Instead, I tend to overthink. *What will people think of me if I do that? Will they misunderstand my motives? Will I end up feeling rejected if I put myself out there?* By the time I've run through my checklist of questions, the moment has passed and I've missed my chance.

As a believer, I know that the Holy Spirit guides me and helps me see opportunities to participate in God's work every day, both in my family and outside of my home. But so often I miss the prompting because I'm too distracted, or worse, I resist it.

For me, the Holy Spirit's nudge often begins as an idea. *You know, this older gentleman I've been talking to in the coffee shop for the last ten minutes?...I should really invite him to church.* This thought is immediately followed by all the reasons I shouldn't do it: *I'm in too much of a hurry. Maybe he already goes to church. Would I seem too pushy or weird for asking?* And if I don't respond to the prompting right away, I generally talk myself out of it. Then I regret *not* doing it for days.

I may have valid reasons for not taking action, but the problem is that I had the chance to participate in what God was doing and I missed it. The Spirit was inspiring action, and I didn't move.

Romans 8:14-15 tells us, "For those who are led by the Spirit of God are the children of God. The Spirit you received does not make you slaves, so that you live in fear again; rather, the Spirit you received brought about your adoption to sonship. And by him we cry, 'Abba, Father.'"

There is freedom and *deep identity* in being led by the Spirit. We are not slaves to our sin, our weaknesses, our fears, our pasts, or our insecurities. Instead, we are beloved daughters of the Most High God. He is our *Abba*—our Daddy. We never have to fear the things He asks us to do.

I wonder if God looks down at us trying to do this dance of being led by the Spirit—so awkward and raw at times—and sees His "Father dreams" for us coming true. He must delight in seeing His children yield to the Holy Spirit and follow His prompting.

Learning to move with the Spirit is a lifetime process. But as His child, you don't have to overthink your every step. You can feel the music, be inspired, and simply move, knowing that your Father finds joy in watching you follow His lead.

Lord, thank You for the gift of the Holy Spirit. Help me let go of my own concerns and insecurities and learn to yield to the Holy Spirit's prompting in every area of my life. Thank You for adopting me as Your child and freeing me from the things that once held me captive. Abba, today I surrender my life and agenda to You. Show me how You want me to move. Amen.

36

Pick Me Up at the Zoo

—— *Gretta* ——

When we lived near Portland, the zoo offered $2 admission on the second Tuesday of every month. We visited as often as we could on a Tuesday because, well, $2 is really hard to beat—and have you seen the price of diapers? The zoo was a fantastic place to spend the day with the kids. We would start out at the otters and massive seals, make our way through the stinky penguin house, and marvel at the bears. The primates were always a hit too. Watching the monkeys swing from branch to branch and the orangutans sit by the big window so you can interact hand to hand between the glass is always magical. Our children loved it. I think the hardest part for me was simply keeping up with their quick little legs as they excitedly ran from animal to animal. And with the baby in the stroller, someone was always on their feet. Running, hopping, wiggling, giggling, exploring, sometimes falling and scraping hands and knees, but always moving, Kaia and Titus experienced it all. They were busy and active and had no intention of slowing down. And really, slowing down and resting was not why we came to the zoo. There was much to see and do.

On one day in particular the trip was wonderful, and everything was going smoothly until just before we arrived at the elephants. As we approached this exhibit, it was touch and go as to whether we would make it at all. The kids started whining so I pulled out snacks from the stroller hoping they just had low blood sugar. But that didn't quite do it. They were just plain tired. They had run a toddler-sized marathon already, and we'd only been there for just over an hour. They had used up all their energy and were running on fumes. Jay and I knew there was so much more to see and experience, so Jay scooped up Kaia, resting her on his shoulders, and I placed Titus on the handle of the stroller to give his legs a break too. We walked for a while like this, made it through the fascinating elephants, and went on through the rest of the zoo. Sometimes the kids walked, but often they rested in our arms.

Our daily journey as mothers is so often like the energy of my children at the zoo. We may start out the day with energy and plans for great things, but soon feel depleted of strength and can't seem to figure out how to make it to bedtime. We need to be carried ourselves. The good news is, God promises to do just that! Isaiah 46:4 says, "I am he; I am he who will sustain you. I have made you and will carry you; I will sustain you and I will rescue you."

The Israelites in these verses were being prepared for deliverance from their captivity in Babylon. Though captivity brought with it some very difficult elements, so did living back on their own in freedom. It was going to take hard work and perseverance to stay true to the calling of following God. Similar to the Israelites, you have been given a high calling that is nearly impossible to do on your own. And God's promise to you is just as powerful as it was to them.

Can you see it all? Let's break this verse down. It starts off by reminding you who is doing the work: God. It's coming from God Himself. The God who made you from nothing. Who designs the most intricate and beautiful creations. So He wants you to keep in mind that this is not an empty promise. He is more than capable. And then look at the three things He's promising: to sustain, carry, and rescue.

To sustain means to comfort, to help and support, or even to hold out for a long time. He sustains you.

To carry means to provide rest for, to lift up, to move, and bear up. He carries you.

To rescue means to save or salvage and liberate. He rescues you.

You see, God will do all these things for you, His daughter. He'll get you through the zoo of your life, whether that zoo is literal or figurative. It's His promise. And Proverbs 30:5 tells us, "God keeps every promise he makes" (GNT).

Believe it or not, you won't be this tired forever. Eventually your children will grow. They will learn to do all the things on their own. They will feed themselves, use the bathroom independently, and yeah, even sleep through the entire night. And you'll wonder how it went so fast. So look at, memorize, and claim this promise from God.

God, thank You for keeping Your promises. When I feel depleted and running on fumes, thank You for the promise that You sustain, carry, and rescue me. As I journey through this day, give me the eyes to see Your hand holding and carrying me through it. Help me see this "zoo" as the blessing it is and give me the energy to carry on. Amen.

37

The Things She Won't Be

—— Suzanne ——

One day, when Sadie was five, we were talking about one of her favorite subjects—weddings. She told me that a girl in her kindergarten class was going to be a flower girl for her aunt's wedding and wear a beautiful dress. "I hope I get to be a flower girl someday," she said.

I told her that I had wished to be a flower girl when I was young too but had never had the opportunity. In fact, the first time I attended a wedding, I was already too old to be a flower girl.

A few months later, I told Sadie the exciting news that we would be attending her cousin's wedding in Colorado. Her eyes widened. "I hope I get to be the flower girl!" she exclaimed, clasping her hands together.

My heart sunk as I thought about how to break the news to her that the flower girl had already been selected. I said, "You know, I think they probably already picked a flower girl—maybe someone who lives close to them." I waited for the disappointment to appear on my girl's face.

Instead, she said, "That's okay. I don't need to be a flower girl. You never were."

I realized in that moment the power of telling my children about my disappointments—the changes in plans and things I had always hoped would happen that didn't. The time I didn't get the lead role in the play but had a great time singing and dancing in the chorus. The time I didn't win a blue ribbon at the fair but still had fun showing my horse. And the time I had to be a single woman for longer than I wanted, but later, at just the right time, I met and married Daddy.

Disappointment is a part of life. When I tell my kids about my own unmet expectations, it frees them. They can breathe a sigh of relief, knowing that it's okay not to get everything you long for or be everything you want to be. Are unmet expectations still painful? Yes. But when we face disappointment, we can trust that God has a purpose in it.

First Corinthians 2:9 says, "'What no eye has seen, what no ear has heard, and what no human mind has conceived'—the things God has prepared for those who love him." I've experienced some loss of dreams during my life, but through it all, I've learned that disappointment is often the beginning of amazing situations and opportunities I never could have imagined. Most of us have endured disappointment of some kind. As our children watch us turn our disappointments into opportunities to trust God, they will do the same.

After Sadie had accepted that she wouldn't be her cousin's flower girl, I said, "You know, it's pretty special that you get to go to your first wedding and sit with Mommy and Daddy."

A huge grin spread across her face. "Yeah," she said dreamily before running off to play. New dreams were already forming in her little heart. She wasn't going to be a flower girl this time, but she felt secure in the knowledge that God had a different plan.

Lord, thank You for preparing wondrous things for me that I never could dream up on my own. Help me point my children to Your goodness and sovereignty. Even now I pray that You would place God-sized dreams in their hearts. I pray that they would see disappointments as opportunities to trust You. Help them know Your great love for them. Amen.

38

Flat Tire!

—— *Gretta* ——

With my three kids buckled in, I started the engine and headed north to my brother's house three hours away in Seattle. My husband was on a manly bonding trip with my dad and two brothers up in Alaska, and while our husbands were gone for the week, my mom and one nearby sister-in-law decided to spend the time together.

About 30 minutes from our destination, my tire blew out. Responding quickly, I pulled the car off to the shoulder just about a half mile after an exit and about 100 feet before the highway narrowed for a bridge. With cars whizzing by at 70 mph (that's 110 kph for my Canadian friends), I sat there nervously trying to figure out my next move. My phone was dead, so I was at the mercy of the passing cars. I thought someone would pull over and help me. After five minutes and no one stopping, I thought maybe if someone saw I had small children then they would offer assistance. So I grabbed almost-two-year-old Titus and held him as I stood outside the car. Surely that would do the trick. But again, no one stopped. After about 20 minutes I began getting really concerned. No one on the crowded highway seemed to notice or care.

I got back into the car and thought I'd give my dead phone a try. I pushed the button, praying it would turn on, and gave a sigh of relief when it lit up. I frantically called my sister-in-law and told her what happened and heard my voice shake and crack as I realized how hopeless I had become. Sternly she said, "Gretta! Hang up now and call 911!" Why I hadn't done that yet is beyond me, but I listened to her and dialed those three numbers. "911. What's your emergency?" I frantically responded, "I have three kids, a flat tire, and I'm just north of exit 114. I need help and my phone is—" That's all I got out before my phone officially died. I just sat there and cried. I didn't know if the dispatcher heard everything, and now officially with no phone, I really *was* stuck. I felt so helpless.

About two minutes later (I'm not kidding) I saw the flashing lights of help. My police officer rescuer called a tow truck who came within a few short minutes, changed my tire in the rushing traffic, and sent me on my way. I couldn't believe how fast help came when I went to the right source.

So often we try to fix our problems ourselves. We may think money or resources, time or people will be able to solve our predicament. But none of those things are the true source of help. This is a lesson Israel had to learn over and over again in the Old Testament. In the book of Isaiah, during one of the many times Israel wasn't following God, they learned firsthand the importance of going to the correct source with the correct motive. And like me, they needed someone to sternly speak to them to get their attention. They tried getting God's favor by going through the motions of obedience, hoping their own ideas would save them. But they had to learn that it was true, heart obedience that was needed. They needed to return to what they had been taught from the beginning, then God will see and help them. Once they humbled themselves and sought true, deep help from God alone, He answered and said, "Then you will call, and the LORD will answer; you will cry for help, and he will say: Here am I" (Isaiah 58:9).

God longs to help when we truly seek Him. He's the true source of help and strength. "Here am I" is His response. As though He's saying, "I was waiting for you to stop trying on your own. I've been waiting for you to want My help. I'm right here, honey."

When I look back at my situation on the side of the highway, I'm pretty stunned by my own stupidity. The real solution (and the easiest one, I might add) was there the whole time. I only needed to humble myself and ask the right source for help.

What problems are you trying to solve on your own? God is waiting for you to truly seek Him and cry for help. Go ahead, dial 911. He's waiting to answer you.

———

God, this is my 911 call to You for help. I'm in over my head and can't fix my problems without You. Thank You for Your promise to help when I humbly call out to You. Amen.

39

Mommy Matters

—— *Suzanne* ——

W e make a good team."
My husband's words came after I had returned home from a weekend birthday getaway with a girlfriend.

"Oh yeah?" I asked, smiling.

"Yeah," he replied. "I don't think I could have held on for much longer without you."

His words surprised me. From my perspective, he'd crushed the whole single-dad thing. He'd balanced work and a babysitter, gotten the older kids off to school each morning, cooked kid-pleasing meals, taken all four to swimming lessons, and even managed to keep the house clean. I was utterly impressed. In fact, from all appearances he'd accomplished more in a single weekend than I could on my best week.

So his affirmation of my importance lifted my spirits and warmed my heart. I don't know about you, but I am so aware of my shortcomings. My inability to tackle those projects I've been meaning to do for months. My lack of patience when my kids want to paint and cut and glitter and smash Play-Doh everywhere. My never-ending struggle to provide nutritious snacks instead of caving and giving them a bowl of choco-puffs...again.

I'm painfully conscious of all the areas where I could be doing better (and they are many). And yet, what I *am doing*—the ways I'm daily investing in my children—is vitally important. In my absence, that became clear to my husband.

In my experience, mom life is basically a steady diet of the thrill of victory and the agony of defeat (sometimes within the same ten-minute period), so it's good to be reminded that what I am doing matters—that I am making a difference. Some days raising young children can seem like a pretty impossible task. But most challenges in life—the ones worth going after—are a process, not something we quickly attain.

Consider Paul's words in Philippians 3:13-14: "Brothers and sisters, I do not consider myself yet to have taken hold of it. But one thing I do: Forgetting what is behind and straining toward what is ahead, I press on toward the goal to win the prize for which God has called me heavenward in Christ Jesus."

Part of my goal as a mom is to raise children who will not only be productive adults but who will love and follow Jesus. While my children will be free to make their own choice whether or not to believe in Him, I want to make that path as appealing and easy to take as possible.

When my role as a mom feels unimportant, I need to remember the goal: I am raising children who I hope and pray will follow Jesus. I stumble at times, but I'm called to just keep moving toward the goal.

Several years ago I ran a half-marathon. During the race, as the sun was beating down on me, I got tired and was tempted to stop. But I just kept going, one foot in front of the other. Being a mom requires similar endurance. When hard days come and I feel like what I'm doing doesn't matter, God says, "Just keep going! You're getting there."

As much as my husband's affirming words blessed me, there are many times when not a living soul notices all that I'm doing—the snuggles, the laundry, the scrubbing, the wiping, the dancing, the dressing, the driving. But my Father in heaven notices. And the One who calls me is cheering me on to get the prize—a prize of inestimable worth.

Lord, some days I feel invisible. Thank You for telling me that what I do matters. Guard my mind from the lie that I am unimportant. Instead, help me forget about mistakes I've made in the past and run with passion toward what is ahead. Amen.

40

Mess Under the Sink

——— Gretta ———

J ay was working at a camp in Oregon when I found myself pregnant with our third child. Our second was only six months old when I took the pregnancy test that turned out to be positive. As I shared the news with a woman at our family camp that summer, she told me not to be surprised when my bathroom looks like it sprouted furry feet from all the gross mildew and grime due to a seriously long time span between scrubbing. I smiled and thanked her for the weird encouragement while simultaneously assuring myself I would never be as bad as "those other moms." I may have three kids in less than three years, but I'll at least scrub the house regularly.

Flash-forward a few short years and I found myself taking the garbage out from under the kitchen sink. As I bent down to tie up the bag, I noticed an odd smell, so I decided to take a few moments to clean the area. And by clean, I mean really scrub. You see, my babies were now old enough to start helping to scrape their plates and put things in the garbage themselves. But as you are fully aware, toddlers are not too reliable when it comes to cleaning up after themselves. So I'm sure it comes as no surprise that this area needed a chisel more than anything.

As I got down on my knees to clean and sanitize under the kitchen sink, I was utterly grossed out! Slowly I worked the grime off the cupboard floor, and it occurred to me it had been at least a full year since it had been wiped down, let alone disinfected. A *year*! So I armed myself with a putty knife (yes, really) and got to work.

And then the voice of my friend echoed in my ears. She warned me this was coming. Sure, she spoke of the bathroom, but it was pretty much the same thing. I was so busy and preoccupied with my crazy life, I hadn't noticed the unaddressed crud build up.

James 5:16 tells us, "Therefore confess your sins to each other and pray for each other so that you may be healed." Sin is a lot like the crud under my sink. It's not really noticeable at first—a quick outburst of annoyance, an unkind word to your spouse. But when left unchecked over time, those small outbursts can build up to create a critical and demanding spirit and can destroy your marriage. Sin prevents us from living the life God intends for us. God's best is that we live in freedom, grace, hope, love, and victory! When sin builds up, we are selfish, bitter, and hurt; we destroy relationships—you name it. But most of all, we hurt our relationship with God.

It's interesting that this verse in James is tucked in among verses about prayer, suffering, and sickness. Sin buildup brings suffering and sickness. Maybe literally, but most often figuratively. Just take a look at what it can do…

- *Suffering:* hurting others and ourselves through unresolved anger and resentment, settling for a cheap version of life instead of living life to the full as God intended.

- *Sickness:* having overinflated views of ourselves, selfishness, and entitlement, among other things.

We are told to confess our sins to one another. Confessing exposes the buildup of crud. It brings it out into the open so we can deal with its reality and allow God to clean it up. It brings freedom, restoration, and healing.

So how are the kitchen cupboards of your life doing? Have you allowed sin to build up unnoticed? When was the last time you did some scrubbing? Be encouraged, Mama, and don't leave your sin one more day to fester and rot. Confess it and move on in health and freedom!

God, please give me the courage to face the crud in my life and begin the process of cleaning it up. I don't want to live with it anymore. Give me trusted friends and wise counsel to share and confess this sin to and help me live in the life You desire for me. Amen.

41

God in My Sorrow

—— *Suzanne* ——

I sat at the end of the examination table in silence. *This is the part where I'm supposed to cry or something,* I thought. Instead, my brain struggled to process the words I'd just heard.

"The baby stopped developing around seven weeks."

According to my calculations, I was nine weeks along. I looked at my husband to see if he'd heard the same thing. His watery eyes confirmed he had.

"What happened?" I asked.

"We can't know," the doctor said gently. "At this early stage, things often just don't match up correctly."

We were days away from a new year and a move from Colorado to California for my husband's new job. And so I began 2016 by packing up 15 years of memories and coming to terms with the fact that there would be no new baby in July. Even though it was too early to tell, I felt sure the baby had been a girl.

A few days before we left Colorado, a gift arrived from my sister. It was a figurine of an angel embracing a small child. When we moved to California, I displayed the angel figurine in a prominent spot with some others I had by the same artist.

At the time of the miscarriage, we didn't tell our other children because they were too young to understand. But about a year after the baby would have been born, my four-year-old daughter was admiring the figurines and asked about the angel. "Is that angel holding Baby Jackson?" she asked, referencing the most recent addition to our family.

"No," I began slowly.

"Is it me?" she asked.

I took a deep breath and decided to tell her. "No, that's a baby who died in Mommy's tummy."

My daughter's eyes widened, and she launched into half a dozen questions: "What happened? Where is the baby now? Was it a boy or a girl?" I told her that we didn't know for sure, but Daddy and I believed the baby was a girl.

Later that day, while riding in the car, Sadie said, "I can't believe I have a sister in heaven! I can't wait to see her someday!" We began to talk about heaven, our imperfect world, and how Jesus came to bring about God's wonderful plan for redemption.

Even though years have passed, every now and then Sadie will still say, "I wish the baby who died in your tummy was here."

"Me too," I'll say. "I'm glad we get to see her again someday."

When I look back on that experience, I am reminded of how deeply I felt God's care through it. The loss was discovered at the perfect time, before we left for California. Family and friends came around us and helped with the packing and cleaning, allowing me to rest. New acquaintances in California reached out with compassion, making the transition easier.

In the midst of my sorrow, God was demonstrating His unfathomable care for me. It reminded me of Jesus' words from Matthew 10:29-31: "Are not two sparrows sold for a penny? Yet not one of them will fall to the ground outside your Father's care. And even the very hairs of your head are all numbered. So don't be afraid; you are worth more than many sparrows."

God cares about the details of our lives, especially the ones that bring us pain. When we first heard our baby had died, I wasn't sure if I would give her a name, as I'd heard of others doing. But a few days after my miscarriage, I awakened in the middle of the night with a name in my mind—a name that had never been on the list for our other two daughters. The next morning I looked up the meaning of the name: *sorrows.*

In the midst of loss, God saw my baby, and He saw me. Though I didn't get to meet her on this earth, my baby's life had significance… even years later, she played a part in her sister's spiritual awakening. I'm so proud to be that little one's mama. And I can't wait to meet her someday. Although I suspect I'll have competition from her sister for the first hug.

Lord, thank You for not only understanding my sorrow but for feeling it with me. Even in times of loss and grief, You are with me and I see You at work. Help me trust in Your great care for me and use my sorrow to draw others to You. Amen.

42

U-Haul and Armor

—— *Gretta* ——

After unloading the moving truck when arriving in Canada with our young family, Jay had three-year-old Kaia accompany him to return the rented U-Haul. They stopped at the gas station on the way to make sure the truck was returned with a full tank of gas. Kaia loved riding in the moving truck. Perched up high in her car seat, she could see all the sights normally blocked by a chair, and she felt like a big, grown-up girl.

As Jay pumped the gas, Kaia sat in her seat admiring her view. He ran to the counter to quickly pay, and while the clerk rang him up, she pointed out the window and said, "Uh, I think your truck is moving." Jay flipped his head toward the door and bolted out, springing toward the U-Haul as it rolled backward across the parking lot, dangerously approaching the wooded ditch drop-off. Adrenaline surging through his body, he flung open the door and dove in headfirst, pressing his hands firmly on the brake pedal. The extra-large U-Haul truck bent the lamp post at the edge of the parking lot and then abruptly stopped just a few feet from the ditch.

Shocked, Jay looked up at Kaia, trying to figure out what just happened. In her sweet three-year-old voice, she said, "You broke it, Daddy."

"*I broke it?*!" Jay couldn't believe what had transpired. With no keys in the ignition and the truck securely in park, how did it roll away? And with his little girl inside, no less?

The police were called and a report was written up. (Jay was thankful he had at least paid the extra money for insurance on the truck.) And less than 48 hours after entering the country, Jay was given his first Canadian ticket. "Welcome to Canada" was all the officer had to say.

It could have been so much worse. As Jay relayed the story to me, we were struck with the reality of what can happen when we let our guard down and get complacent. Jay thought, as I and many others often do, that he could just run in and pay really quick and leave Kaia in the truck. I mean, we all know how long it takes to get a toddler in and out of a vehicle. And Jay knew he was just going to be a minute.

But that's all it takes sometimes. Our enemy is searching constantly for someone he can devour and destroy. He is just waiting for us to let our guard down. This is why it's essential for us to be strong, mighty, warrior women. Paul, in Ephesians, tells us why we need to stand firm and be strong in the Lord. Ephesians 6:10-12 says, "Finally, be strong in the Lord and in his mighty power. Put on the full armor of God, so that you can take your stand against the devil's schemes. For our struggle is not against flesh and blood, but against the rulers, against the authorities, against the powers of this dark world and against the spiritual forces of evil in the heavenly realms."

I'm not sure what you think after reading those verses, but I know they give me a reality check about some of the struggles I face on a daily basis. There is a battle being fought that I cannot see. But it's a battle I am told how to fight. Paul's words about standing firm to fight come after he talks about our need to be unified as Christians and our responsibility to change our thinking and behaviors. He gives us guidelines as husbands, wives, children, parents, workers, and managers. Basically, how to live in every aspect of life. So after all that, Paul says (and I'm paraphrasing now), "Oh yeah, by the way, in order to live like that, you'll need to fight and be strong in the Lord."

The good news is that you're not left to fight alone with your own strength. There is an armor God gives us to use. An armor that will enable you to stand firm, to have the relationships that honor God and those around you, and to fight against the evil that seeks to destroy you.

But you must be attentive and actively fight for it. You cannot cut corners and run into the store to pay for gas, leaving your child in the car, so to speak. With an enemy lurking, you must be vigilant. You must put on:

- A belt of truth,
- A breastplate of righteousness,
- A shield of faith,
- Footwear of readiness with the gospel of peace,
- A helmet of salvation,
- A sword of the Spirit,
- And prayer.

These are your armor pieces to give you the strength to stand firm. Read through that list again. Truth. Righteousness. Faith. Peace. Salvation. God's Word. Prayer. All working together to keep you strong in God's mighty power.

Don't cut corners. Put on your armor daily. And fight for your relationships. Fight for godliness.

God, help me be a warrior who is ready to fight for Your best in my life. Give me Your mighty power like You promise in Ephesians. Give me the strength and wisdom to understand that Your enemies are trying to destroy this life. Thank You for giving me everything I need to overcome. Amen.

43

Avoiding the Rot of Envy

—— *Suzanne* ——

I scroll through my feed and the green-eyed monster rears its ugly head again: *jealousy.* Deep down, I know they're just mamas like me who are proud of their babies or their husbands (or that they made it out of the house to a place worth talking about!), but the pang is still there, gnawing at the pit of my stomach like a flesh-eating virus.

Is her life better than mine? Is she a more patient, kind, wise, cool (fill-in-the-blank) mom than I am? Are her kids turning out nicer than mine? Is her husband more pleased with her? Does she have more friends?

The real me would never begrudge another mom her successes or even sharing them on social media. I once posted a picture of muffins I'd baked (pumpkin with streusel topping) just to prove that I *do something* useful with my day other than attempt to tame the ever-growing laundry pile. The post was a desperate cry into the void: "See? I'm valuable! I make things. I do things. I'm not just a person who used to have an interesting life, who now stays at home all day wiping bottoms and dreaming up ways to get little people to eat vegetables."

It's hard to admit, but sometimes my life feels pretty insignificant. And seeing pictures of other moms doing things right tends to feed my own insecurities that I'm doing things wrong. You may not relate to my examples here, but I'm sure you have your own insecurities. Maybe you're an organized, domestic diva, but posts about romantic husband gestures you know will never come your way get you down. Or it could be you have the greatest love story ever told with your spouse, but you ache over seeing others invited and included when you're not. Or maybe your troubles don't even arise from an online source but from seeing other moms out and about who seem to have more going for them than you do.

I think we would all agree that the glimpses we get into the lives of others are mostly their successes. The brilliant teacher gift they concocted. The special outing they took with their child. The adorable matching outfits they were able to coerce their little ones into wearing. The home renovations that look like HGTV stopped by. But let's face it, no one wants to post about the possibility that a hazmat team may show up at their door later if something isn't done about the condition of their house.

Proverbs 14:30 says, "A tranquil heart gives life to the flesh, but envy makes the bones rot" (ESV). Isn't that a perfect description of how it feels to envy? Like my bones are rotting. Like the marrow of *my life* is decomposing as I fixate on the good things others possess. *Gross!*

So how can I get this tranquil life-giving heart? Scripture is pretty clear that the key lies in focusing less on my own perceived successes (or failures), and instead praising Him for the unique ways He has gifted me and is working in my life. That begins with thanking Him for the gift of salvation and the immeasurable benefits that come with it.

As I spend more time reminding myself of who God is and who I am as His child—significant, loved, blessed with every spiritual blessing, equipped, supported, *seen*—I will have a harder time pining away for what others have. And when I do feel that twinge as I observe another mama's blessings, I can take the opportunity to say a prayer for her or reach out to share a cup of coffee. Because what better way to share in one another's successes (and messes) than to get off the screen and into each other's lives.

Lord, I confess that I'm sometimes envious when I see the successes of others. Please forgive me for failing to recognize the many good gifts You have given me. Today, help me focus on my identity as Your child. Help me learn to celebrate the successes of others and find ways to support those who may be feeling insignificant. Thank You for calling me to the amazing task of being a mom. Amen.

44

The Worst Five Minutes Ever

—— *Gretta* ——

As a mom of littles, I often kept my sanity by cooking with my toddlers. We would pull a chair into the kitchen, and they would stand beside me and help pour, mix, and nibble as we went along. One day we were by the stove carefully watching the noodles boil for macaroni and cheese. As soon as the noodles were cooked, I removed the pan from the stove and poured the noodles into the strainer in the sink. The next step was to add the milk and butter. That's when I realized I needed butter from the extra fridge in the basement.

Twenty seconds later, I kid you not, I was hurrying back up the stairs when I heard a blood-curdling scream. My two-year-old had done the thing all mothers fear. The palm of his hand had three very clear burn rings on it from the still-hot element. I ran cold water over his hand and sat down on the couch, pressing a bag of frozen peas on his chubby palm.

That's when I heard the splashing noise coming from the bathroom. I went to investigate and found my 11-month-old standing at the toilet happily squishing poo between his fingers! Upon closer inspection I could see the brown goo all over his arms and legs.

Horrified, I placed my 11-month-old in the empty bathtub. (I would have rather hosed him off, but it was January and that seemed a bit cruel.) That's when I heard a loud *pop!* and my three-year-old's sweet voice saying, "Uh-oh, Mama. I'm sorry."

I walked back to the living room to find my daughter looking at the laptop on the floor that she had just stepped on—forever destroying the screen. In five minutes I had gone from happily preparing lunch for my littles to crying in a heap with two of the three of them. (The third was still in poo heaven.)

My whole life I've heard that God will never give me more than I can handle. But in all my dreaming about raising a family, I never imagined a scenario like this. In that moment I just wanted to crawl into a ball, call my own mother, and give away my children. This parenting stuff was tough! But the truth is, God never actually promises to *only* give us what we can handle. (That phrase actually comes from a passage talking about temptation—a topic for another time.)

Instead, God promises He will always be with us. He walks with us through our suffering. He carries our burdens. We were never designed to "handle" this life without Him. I know there are times you feel alone. I did. On days like the one described here, it's a wonder I didn't throw in the towel.

Take heart, warrior Mama! You are not the first person in history to need a reminder of God's promises. Long ago the people of Israel felt defeated. Babylon had conquered their nation, exiling them far from home. They felt alone, forgotten, and hopeless. Ever been there? Read what God said to His chosen people in Isaiah 41:10:

> Fear not, for I am with you; be not dismayed, for I am your God; I will strengthen you, yes, I will help you, I will uphold you with My righteous right hand (NKJV).

Read that again out loud. Do you hear all those promises?

1. I am with you.
2. I am your God.
3. I will strengthen you.
4. I will help you.
5. I will hold you up with my righteous right hand.

In one verse, God gives such amazing and timely promises of comfort and hope. Take heart. You have the almighty God of the universe *with* you, *strengthening* you, *helping* you, and *upholding* you. No matter what comes your way, you are not alone.

So when you find yourself crying on the couch, tenderly nursing wounds, or cleaning up poop for the umpteenth time, remember these promises and take courage.

———————

Lord, no matter what the kids throw at me today, help me remember You are with me in the midst of it. You are strong and mighty. Remind me that You will strengthen me with what I need for today. You are the Great Helper, and You want to help and uphold me. Please bring that to my mind when I feel like giving up. Thank You for Your promises. Amen.

45

Heart of Acceptance

—— *Suzanne* ——

My seven-year-old dances around the karate dojo, throwing back his head and flailing his arms. We are at a friend's birthday party, and Josiah is exploring his new surroundings by wandering around the blue plastic mat, quoting his favorite TV show.

I tell him to go join the others for the karate lesson and he does. The other children line up facing the sensei. After a few seconds, Josiah bounds away from the group. "Mommy!" he yells. "I like this place!"

His actions are no surprise to me, but the sensei calls out to him gruffly, "Big boy! Stand on the line with the others. You need to show respect here!"

"Okay!" Josiah says cheerfully, having no idea he's being reprimanded.

That's when I get a lump in my throat. My son is almost always surrounded by the safety of people who know him, and his huge smile and sweet personality quickly win everyone over. But this situation is a painful reminder that his developmental disabilities make him different. He doesn't fit the mold. He will always process his world in a vastly different way from other kids.

Deep down, I know he is who God has made him to be. But a part of me grieves for what he's not. And truth be told, Josiah isn't the only one of my children I struggle to accept. There are quirks about each child that challenge me at times. I wish one would be more outgoing. I wish another would show more self-restraint in public or control her emotions better. And the baby, well, he's perfect for now, but as he grows and develops, I'm sure he'll have foibles too.

Here's what I'm realizing: My children are not me. They won't think exactly the same way I do or make the same choices (even if they had my maturity). And while that may cause frustration and make it hard for me to accept them at times, the way they express their individuality is actually beautiful.

In Psalm 139:14, David says, "I praise you because I am fearfully and wonderfully made; your works are wonderful, I know that full well." God created each of my children with unique personalities, attributes, and abilities to build His kingdom—a kingdom built on acceptance. Romans 15:7 says, "Accept one another, then, just as Christ accepted you, in order to bring praise to God."

One of our roles as mamas is to accept our children the way Christ accepts us. When we do, it brings praise to God, who created each child in amazing detail. Moms are known for loving their kids unconditionally. But just because God has called us to model His acceptance to our kids doesn't mean we'll do that perfectly. We *need* His help every day to show our kids that they are accepted for who they are—by us, but more importantly by Him.

As I watched the joy on my son's face as he explored the dojo, I realized I was the one who needed to work on acceptance. On the way home I heard his excited voice from the back seat: "Thanks for taking me, Mom. I liked that place!" I smiled at my sweet, thoughtful boy's words. What had been uncomfortable for me had been an amazing new adventure for him. He had taken a few more steps toward finding his way in the world. And as I learn to open my eyes to who God has made my children to be, I can enable them to walk the unique paths God has designed for them.

Lord, thank You that my children are fearfully and wonderfully made. Help me appreciate who You have made them to be and guide them into the specific callings You have placed on their lives. Help me love them even when they fail to meet my expectations. Help me accept them the way You accept me. Amen.

46

Gaining Gratitude

—— *Gretta* ——

I started the thankful leaves our second November in Canada. Koen was not yet two and had a total of three words in his repertoire so he didn't participate, but the other kids fully embraced it. Canadians celebrate Thanksgiving in October, and though the traditional meal and the focus on thankfulness are the same as it is in the States, it's not nearly as big of a holiday as it is for Americans. When we moved to Canada, I informed Jay that we would always celebrate American Thanksgiving as well, and the "thankful leaves" were my attempt at making the holiday special for the kids.

I cut out construction paper leaves, and every day I'd ask Kaia and Titus what they were thankful for. Words like *bunny* and *taggie* (their most special possessions) came out, so that's what I wrote down on their leaves. They also came up with people's names, and all sorts of seemingly random items—snakes, hot dogs, clouds, slides—are also included in the leaves. Throughout the month we added daily our thanks and then taped the leaves all over the windows. As they grew, they drew pictures and eventually wrote their own messages. We repeat this tradition every year, and I save the leaves from year to year, eager each November to pull them out again and reread the messages.

When we practice gratefulness, we're trading complaints for thanks.

We give up sorrow for joy. And we recognize our blessings instead of our burdens.

Cultivating an attitude of gratitude can be difficult, but it's worth the hard work. Paul tells us in 1 Thessalonians 5:18 to "give thanks in all circumstances; for this is God's will for you in Christ Jesus." Admittedly, it's harder than it looks. When the kids are crying and won't share their space, I struggle being thankful. When I spend an hour of my precious time cooking dinner only to have everyone turn their nose up at it, gratitude is not the first emotion I experience. I'm pretty sure annoyance and frustration are my initial go-tos when it comes to situations like these. I prefer my life to be beautifully pleasant. You know, everyone getting along, getting enough sleep to easily manage my day, a kitchen with no dirty dishes, and a house that cleans itself. That certainly can't be too much to ask, can it? I'm sure it would be easy to be thankful then, right?

But that's not what Paul tells us. He doesn't say, "Be thankful when everything is going your way." He also doesn't say, "Be thankful when you are happy." Paul has the audacity to tell you and me to be thankful in *every* circumstance. That means when the sink and kitchen counter are full of dirty dishes, I make the deliberate choice to be thankful that we had food to eat. When my home resembles a tornado zone, I choose to see the remnants of children playing. And when the fatigue sets in because I only sleep in three-hour increments, I can look at my baby, realize he won't be this small forever, and be grateful for the gift of being his mama.

It's not always easy, and sometimes I really have to be creative to find a way to turn my situation into gratitude, but every time I do (yes, every time), I am not only more pleasant to be around, I am also more aware of God's active presence in my life.

I need reminders to help me be thankful always. A friend once told me about a thankful journal she had. It was such a simple, small reminder for her to think differently. So I picked up a small notebook and keep it in my purse. I just write one liners of gratitude. Things like "a sunny day" or "giggles from a two-year-old" or even "dandelions from Koen" are among the things for which I am grateful.

Being thankful is for more than one holiday per year. It's a way of life…in every circumstance. A grateful heart is a happy heart (Psalm 28:7), and a grateful heart points others to God (Psalm 34:1-3). I don't know about you, but I'd love to have a happy heart that points others to God. You can do it. We can do it together. What can you be grateful for in this moment? Today? This month? This year? No matter what is going on, develop a lifestyle of gratitude and be thankful…always.

Dear God, thank You for all the amazing blessings in my life. As I look around me, there really is so much to be grateful for. Help me develop a lifestyle of gratitude and always see the blessings around me…even when it's difficult. Amen.

47

Beauty in Diversity

—— *Suzanne* ——

I began noticing personality differences between my own children around the time my third child, Amelia, began showing her own distinct personality. But it wasn't until I volunteered in Sadie's kindergarten class that I saw how *very* different children can be.

I observed as a table of eight children around the same age completed a writing worksheet. Some paid steady attention to their task, completing each step with utmost care. Others dove into the coloring portions of their worksheets before tackling the academic bits. Some barely worked, preferring to chat with their neighbors. Still others constantly noticed which of their peers needed something and would quickly deliver a glue stick or pencil to a student in need. Watching them, I marveled at how intrinsically different each child was.

Even art pieces where the children had used bingo markers to make 100 dots in the shape of a large circle varied greatly. Some had a pattern. Others appeared to be completely random. Some were two-tone, while others utilized every color of the rainbow. No two were the same.

As I observed these little ones, all born within the same year, I marveled at how God had created each one unique. Different personalities. Different abilities. Different preferences. One day many of them will be moms and dads. And they won't all be the same then either.

For some reason it's easy for me to see children and recognize how God has made each one different. But as a mom, I'm tempted to compare when I see another parent doing things differently, or better, than I'm doing them. I see the mom who's great at staying on task and lament because my to-do list is always overflowing. Or I notice the mama with a gift for rushing in when someone is in need, and I feel like a loser that I didn't think of that! But just like those kindergarten students, each of us mamas is different. And the cool part is, it's by design.

Listen to what 1 Corinthians 12:18-22 says about our diversity:

> But in fact God has placed the parts in the body, every one of them, just as he wanted them to be. If they were all one part, where would the body be? As it is, there are many parts, but one body. The eye cannot say to the hand, "I don't need you!" And the head cannot say to the feet, "I don't need you!" On the contrary, those parts of the body that seem to be weaker are indispensable.

In this passage, Paul is talking about the Christians who form the church—all believers everywhere who are the hands and feet of Jesus on earth. And the big point here is that our differences are intentional because, like parts of the body, we're meant to work together. I don't know about you, but I have often felt like the weaker part of the body. And yet this passage tells me that I am indispensable. *You* are indispensable.

God has placed you exactly where He wants you to be. Just as my daughter's teacher intentionally arranged the groups of children at each table to function well together, God has placed you in the exact seat where you belong. You are in the place where He can most effectively use your personality, abilities, and preferences.

As I marveled at God's creativity among these little people, whose personalities and gifts were still emerging, I thought of myself as a child. Many of the strengths I had then, such as a creative mind, compassionate spirit, and commitment to sticking with a project, are areas where I now shine as a mom. How freeing to know that God designed me with intention and has placed me exactly where I need to be. And the same is true for you.

———————

Lord, I am in awe of the diversity of Your creation. I see Your creativity displayed in my children and even in me as a mom. Help me embrace who You have made me to be. Instead of comparing myself to others, help me depend on those who are strong where I am weak and glorify You through my specific design. Amen.

48

Joy Found in the Orange Juice

—— *Gretta* ——

My husband has a great affinity for orange juice, preferably without pulp. As newlyweds I'd occasionally sneak a cup of the sweet drink onto the bathroom counter while he was in the shower as a little loving surprise. I'd put my best stealth-mode into action and my goal was always to place it undetected, and I'd usually giggle a bit when I knew I had succeeded in my task. He called me the orange juice fairy.

When Kaia was two, I gave her my fairy wings and she carried on the tradition. And when the boys "came of age," they too joined in the fun as orange juice warriors. I taught them all how to walk into the bathroom quietly and carefully place the cup on the counter unnoticed. Once the kids entered the picture, the fairy tale really began. Jay made up a story about an enchanted fairyland beyond the sea where fairies and warriors lived. The orange juice was gathered from either the tallest trees in the land or from the spring where juice simply poured forth. It was a magical story. A story each of the kids delighted in hearing and imagining their part.

But the icing on the cake was how every single time Jay emerged from the shower to see a carefully placed glass of orange juice sitting on the counter, he'd get dressed and then call out with great excitement,

"Kids! Come quick! The orange juice fairy/warrior was here!" Of course they came running, giggling the whole way, to see the beloved drink. With great joy and fanfare they'd all have a taste and discuss where they believed the fairy or warrior harvested the juice. It was a delightful game. The kids delighted in "surprising" Daddy nearly as much as their daddy delighted in their interaction together. That's what was happening. The greatness wasn't about the orange juice at all. Jay is a grown man and can purchase, make, and get his own orange juice. Rather, it was about the kids and how much he loved them.

When I became a parent, my understanding and view of God grew deeper regarding Him as my Father. "He will take great delight in you; in his love he will no longer rebuke you, but will rejoice over you with singing" (Zephaniah 3:17). What a lovely verse!

In a society where the word *father* has many meanings and invokes a myriad of emotions, it can be difficult to understand or accept that God the Father actually takes delight in you. We have all grown up with an idea of what *Father* means. For some, a father protects, encourages, directs, and provides. But sadly, you may associate father with abuse, abandonment, emotionally absent, and demanding. If that is your story, God wants to transform your thinking. As your Father, God delights in you. He protects you. He loves you. No matter what your struggles in life, no matter who you think you are or what you have done, no matter your financial status or your parenting abilities, God longs for you to know:

- He takes great delight in you. Great delight. He enjoys watching you and spending time with you.

- He does not rebuke you. In fact, He "quiets you with His love" (NKJV). His love calms and brings you security and peace.

- He rejoices over you with singing.

Can you just see it? He is so filled with joy because of *you* that He can't help but sing!

Does this change your understanding of how God thinks of you? I personally just love this picture of my heavenly Father fully and completely enthralled with His children. Have you seen that before? His love, His delight, His peace, and His joy are so great for you. Just as you love your babies, God loves you immensely more. So take that with you today as you clean, change diapers, and wipe tears. Imagine your heavenly Father doing the same for you, with great joy. You are, after all, His baby girl.

———————

God, thank You for loving me. Thank You for delighting in me. It's hard to imagine sometimes how You can, but please help me see what You see. Give me the quietness of spirit to receive Your joy and delight. Amen.

49

Making Mom Friends

—— Suzanne ——

M y first semester of college was brutal. I was a studious introvert from a small town attending college in the big city.
Everything about college overwhelmed me: the classes, the
professors, my early-morning campus job, and especially all the people. In fact, I pretty much gave up on having friends during those first
few months.

Gretta, who was my roommate, was the opposite. An extrovert in
every sense of the word, she excelled at relationships and always made
time for her friends. On top of her job at a burger joint and managing
her studies, she often hung out with her friends late into the night. At
the end of that first semester, during finals week, I actually made some
of her friends my own when she invited me to their makeshift Christmas party at an all-night diner. (I'm forever grateful for that charita-
ble act.)

Over the years, I was able to push outside of my comfort zone and
make some friendships I have to this day. My relational style is of the
slow-burn variety, but once we're friends I'm extremely loyal.

By my junior year, I finally felt connected. One night I went to a
coffee shop to do some homework. I recognized the barista who took
my order as someone I'd shared a class with the year before, but I was

too shy to say anything. As I opened my wallet to pay for my coffee, he said, "Do you go to Multnomah?"

I smiled. I'd finally arrived. Someone knew me!

"Yes!" I said.

"Oh," he said, grinning. "I saw the picture of Gretta in your wallet." I looked down, and sure enough, there was a little wallet snap of two smiling roomies. Gretta and I still laugh about that story and how well it defines each of our personalities.

Despite being fairly low-profile, I came out of college with some dear friends. And when I moved to Colorado and started my career, I met some women who would eventually become lifelong friends.

Then I became a mom.

I was in my thirties when my oldest was born, and I felt like I was back at square one when it came to relationships. I was a pro at coffee dates, but I had no idea how to do playdates. I had loved being part of my comedy improv group but hadn't a clue about being part of a moms' group. Frankly, I felt awkward and had no idea how to connect in this new sphere.

At first I did what I did my freshman year of college. I stayed home a lot and focused on learning to parent an infant. Because I'm an introvert, I didn't crave relationship beyond my husband and talking to my sister or mom on the phone. But over time, I noticed something. I was lacking a support system. I needed friends.

The Bible is clear that we need people to encourage us, support us, and strengthen us. Proverbs 27:17 says, "As iron sharpens iron, so one man sharpens another." To be the best mom I can be, I need other women in my life. And though my personality may make it more difficult for me to connect at times, Proverbs 18:24 says, "A man of many companions may come to ruin, but there is a friend who sticks closer than a brother" (ESV).

I don't need dozens of friends. I just need a few committed allies who encourage me to grow and be the best version of myself. And through the years I've found ways that work best for me to connect. I set up evening coffee dates with new mom friends so our first conversation can be uninterrupted. Instead of doing lots of things during the week when I'm managing my kids' activities, my husband and I team up on weekends to host families for dinner. I attend an evening Bible study, when Kevin can put the kids to bed, so I don't have the stress of loading up my kids for childcare.

Making friends in the mom years requires resourcefulness and tenacity, but the payoff is worth it. I may have gotten off to a rocky start in college, but the friendships I eventually formed made my life infinitely better. And the same is true of the friends I make during these years. They will add to my journey in ways I never could imagine.

————————

Lord, thank You for creating me for friendship. Thank You for the women You've brought into my life during each season who have molded me into the person I am today. Give me the courage to reach outside myself to pursue authentic community and build friendships in the way I'm designed to do that. Show me someone I can befriend today. Amen.

50

The Extroverted Mama

———— Gretta ————

Whenever I introduce myself to a new group of people, I tend to share interests of mine, like, "I love coffee, I have three kids, I've been married 'x' number of years, and my favorite thing is just being with people." It's true. Unlike what Suzanne describes, *my* happy place always, yes, *always*, involves friends. Outside, inside, hiking, or sitting on the couch together mugs in hand, I love people.

On one of my first dates with my husband we went to the symphony. I was happy to share my love of classical music with my boyfriend of two weeks, but at intermission I made friends with the women sitting next to me in the concert hall. Jay informed me at the end of the concert that I spoke more to the strangers than I did to him! It had never occurred to me *not* to talk to complete strangers. I mean, they were sitting next to me, after all. I find the world so much more enjoyable when I can talk to everyone in it. I am an off-the-charts extrovert.

Less than a year after our symphony date, Jay and I married. During our first year of marriage we spent most of our non-working hours hunkered down at home enjoying life as newlyweds. We rarely went out because we were blissfully loving being just us. But one by one as the children joined our family, I seemed to struggle more and more with finding time to be with others. It got harder to leave the house, so I stayed home most days. I left to get food, go to the park on a nice day, and take the kids to their well-baby checkups. In fact, I think I saw my doctor more regularly than almost anyone else. Gone were the days of hanging out with friends and enjoying long phone conversations.

Jay would come home from a long day at work and just want to unwind by himself. I had been home alone with the littles all day and just wanted to talk and hang out. Though I was surrounded by my family, I quickly became lonely and somewhat irritable. My loneliness wasn't from postpartum depression, and it wasn't because I didn't love my littles or my husband. My loneliness was simply because I am energized by relationships.

Hebrews 12:14 says to "make every effort to live in peace with everyone and to be holy." I was having a difficult time living at peace with just the one man I share a bed with; how could I possibly live at peace with everyone?! I realized that for me to live in peace with even just those in my own household, I needed to figure out how to see friends more regularly.

When reading through Paul's letters to the early churches, I became convinced that he too was an extrovert. Everywhere he went, he built relationships. In all of his letters he greets people by name, encouraging them and thanking them for their part in spreading the gospel. And sprinkled throughout his letters are messages on how to treat one another, the importance of our differences in the body of Christ, and how to love.

So, as an extroverted woman, I learned I needed to be more creative in finding my people time. I made friends with other moms I met through church, and we got together weekly at one another's homes while our toddlers played together. I hung out longer after church service to visit with as many people as possible. My husband and I joined a life group that met weekly, and I got adult people time then. I started attending a mom's group at another church every other week. I noticed that as I ventured out to these various places and had contact with people over the age of five, I came home more energized and more myself.

Are you a people person wondering how to live at peace with those around you when you are depleted of all your energy? Let me encourage you to look for ways to connect outside your home. Or maybe open your own home, mess and all, to someone else who may be struggling just like you. If you are an extrovert, I promise you will find your personality begin to return and you will be able to live more peaceably with those around you.

———————

God, I hadn't realized how badly I need to be with people! Please show me how and where to find other adults to share life with so I don't feel so alone. I long for grown-up conversation. Give me wisdom and friendship so I can function as You have designed me to be. Amen.

51

Giving Up Control

—— *Suzanne* ——

I've always been a fairly goal-oriented person. And growing up, I did well in school and found at least moderate success in most of my pursuits. Gretta could probably comment on how my driven, perfectionist tendencies affected her during college. Late nights of me studying while she tried to sleep. Me hogging our room for homework time while she spent time with friends. I'll admit, my performance mode was sometimes in overdrive.

For a long time, I was able to control my life by working hard and being prepared. But at the end of college, I developed an autoimmune condition that almost forced me to quit my classes and move home. As painful as that experience was, God used it to show me that I actually *didn't* have control of my life and that I *couldn't* guarantee success through my own efforts. While I didn't like that fact, it was freeing to be reminded of Who *did* have control.

My health eventually improved, and as my strength grew, some of my control tendencies returned. That was fine in an eight-to-five work environment where my life ran pretty much like clockwork. Then I had my first child.

As a young mom, I found my life becoming increasingly more

difficult to control. After all, I couldn't predict when the baby would have a blowout or cry for an hour in the middle of the night. And when my seven-month-old son ended up in the hospital, I realized I couldn't even control my child's health.

I was struggling to gain control over the unpredictable elements of my life, and another area of my life that felt out of control was my time with God.

That's when the *I shoulds* started.

I should wake up earlier to do my devotions.

I should make the time to pray.

I should have more patience.

I should choose joy.

I should…I should…I should.

My ambitions rose from a noble place; I *knew* I needed Jesus more than ever. I needed to feel His love and presence daily. I needed Him to empower me to do all the things motherhood required. I needed His help to raise these adorable (and at times exasperating) little image-bearers of His.

In the Old Testament, we read about a man named Zerubbabel, who was called by God to rebuild the temple following the Babylonian exile. In Zechariah 4:6, the prophet speaks powerful words from God: "This is the word of the LORD to Zerubbabel: 'Not by might nor by power, but by my Spirit,' says the LORD Almighty."

That's an important message for me too. God has given me the task of raising children who love and serve Him. At times, this task feels impossible. And my default mode is to make a list and do things by my own might and power—which is so often in short supply. But God tells me, "No, this isn't going to happen by might or power. This is going to happen by *My Spirit* working in and through you!"

Mama, you don't have to live in the guilt-inducing world of *I shoulds*. God calls you to lay aside your own might and determination and rely on His Spirit to give you what you need.

When I realized that I was in a slump, I started doing *something* every day. I listened to worship music while I was driving. I caught a sermon or podcast while I cleaned the kitchen. I read to my toddler out of our storybook Bible and talked to her about my wonderful God and the things He had done in Mommy's life.

As I gave up my desire to have control and somehow make every aspect of my life perfect, God met me there. He gave me an extra portion of strength and joy. He showed me things I could be grateful for. He opened my eyes to how He was working in the mundane aspects of my life. I still had moments where I tried to gain control in my own strength, but when I looked to God instead, I accomplished more than I thought possible. More than that, He accomplished His work in me.

Lord, I confess that I sometimes try to do things in my own power; my resources so often fall short. When I feel overwhelmed and out of control, help me look to You. My own might can never fix all of my problems. Help me replace it with total dependence on You. Accomplish Your will and work in me today. Amen.

52

Redwoods and the Epic Stomach Flu

———— *Gretta* ————

Not long ago, Jay was on a work trip and gone for a week. The day he left, all three kids and I came down with an epic stomach flu. It was all the horrors you could imagine and worse. The dishes piled up. The laundry (oh, that never-ending mountain) reached unprecedented heights. It was gross and downright horrible.

At the same time we had a friend doing some minor construction work at the house. When he came back from his lunch break, my youngest, Koen, was crying in his crib, Kaia sat in the bathroom calling for help, and I stood (still in my pajamas) over my middle child, Titus, who had just vomited all over the living room floor. To say it was a low point would be an understatement.

My friend had entered a viral warzone. Looking shell-shocked, he said, "I don't think I should do any more work today." And with that, he walked out the door. I thought for sure he had decided to save himself while there was still time, but to my surprise, he returned half an hour later with two cans of chicken noodle soup and some 7Up. He had also alerted some people of the situation at the camp where Jay works. That afternoon I had three more visitors who brought me soup, ginger ale, tea, medicine, apple juice, and Popsicles. Each time I answered the door, I stood there crying in my pajamas, hair in a pony-tail, no makeup.

This situation, oddly enough, reminded me of the coastal redwood trees of Northern California. Redwoods are larger than life. If you ever want to feel like a tiny ant, just walk among them for even five minutes.

The coastal redwoods of Northern California may be huge, but they desperately need each other. In order for them to withstand the high winds and storms that constantly pass through, their roots spider out 100 feet from the trunk! *One hundred feet!* Because the soil along the coastline is wet, the roots cannot go down deep. So in order for the tree to survive, the roots grow wide. And as they grow wide, they inter-twine with the other trees also growing wide. So in a forest, every tree supports the trees around it—in a 100-foot radius. This is how they withstand the storms.

The love and care pouring out from my root system that day held me up through one of the hardest weeks of my life. By the time Jay came home, we were on the mend and the house was back to its nor-mal level of chaos. He managed to dodge the worst of it. And that was okay, because I had my roots spread wide.

Just like the redwoods, we were designed to need support from those around us. God designed us in His image for relationship. First Thessalonians 5:11 tells us to "encourage one another and build each other up." My friends bringing soup and medicine gave me needed encouragement at just the right time. Hebrews 10:24 says, "Let us think of ways to motivate one another to acts of love and good works" (NLT). My friend telling others of my need activated a chain reaction that helped me through a hard time.

These verses aren't just happy suggestions for a better life. They tap into God's very design for us. This is His best. To encourage. To build up. To motivate to godly action. Doing these things requires being vul-nerable and sensitive to the needs around us.

Sometimes having wide roots means supporting your friend by tak-ing her kids to the park so she can have a nap. And then there are the moments when your wide roots leave you crying in your pajamas at your front door while others bless you. That's how it works. You give.

You receive. You support and are supported. Without your root system, you fall over when the storms come. So follow the example of the giant redwoods and spread your roots. Because believe me—you're going to need them.

————————

Lord, You know how desperately I need support. Thank You for providing other believers to be a root system and hold me up when the storms of life come. Sometimes it can be so hard to accept help, but as I look to help the needs around me, give me the humility to accept it when it's my turn to receive. Thank You. Amen.

53

My Fanciest Dress

——— Suzanne ———

After my third child in four years was born, I hit an all-time low in the area of body image. I'd put on about ten additional pounds per pregnancy that I was having a hard time shedding. One day Sadie and I were looking through wedding photos, one of her favorite things to do.

"Why don't you wear your fanciest dress, Mom?" my three-year-old asked, referring to my wedding dress. I could have answered that women typically don't wear their wedding dresses after the big day, but for some reason I said, "It doesn't fit anymore."

Being well-acquainted with this phenomenon in her own life, she wrinkled her nose and said, "Because you got bigger?"

"Yes," I said, stifling a sigh. "I got bigger when babies were growing in my tummy."

Her eyes sparkled with excitement as she said, "And I was one of the babies that grew in your tummy and made you bigger?"

Her enthusiasm choked me up. To me, my inability to lose the baby weight was a point of shame and failure. To my little girl, it was all joy that I got bigger because it brought about our family!

I needed to hear my daughter's perspective. Of course I wanted to get fit and be healthy for my family. But God had given me a strong—albeit *bigger*—body that He used to bring about three, and eventually four, little miracles. That was something worth getting excited about!

Psalm 13:6 proclaims, "I will sing the LORD's praise, for he has been good to me." I'm sure I'm not the only mama who can point to example after example of God's goodness. He allowed me to meet my wonderful husband after over a decade of being a single adult. He blessed me with four beautiful children. He has made my work fruitful, even while balancing the pressures of being a stay-at-home mom.

Despite all of those blessings, I so often focus on the imperfect areas of my life and allow them to pull my focus away from the significant things God is doing. Sadie easily recognized God's goodness and plan in the very thing I perceived as a flaw. And praise for what He had done bubbled up in her little heart!

Maybe a failure or inadequacy is getting you down today. Make a mental list of the ways God has been good to you, even in the past 24 hours. Psalm 34:8 says, "Taste and see that the LORD is good." Tangible evidences of God's generosity and goodness are everywhere—even in the excess weight or the overflowing laundry basket or the bottomless sink of dishes.

I would love to get back into my "fanciest dress" one day. But in the meantime, I want to learn to see God's goodness the way my daughter does and praise Him for it. He has done great things.

————

Lord, thank You for Your goodness. You have done wondrous things in my life. I'm sorry for the times I've fixed my eyes on my own flaws instead of praising You for the many blessings in my life. Help me recognize Your goodness each day. Amen.

54

Peace in the Chaos

———— Gretta ————

We were walking along the boardwalk in our small town, just me and Titus. Living by the ocean means we can get some crazy storms, but it also means some days are simply stunning. As we walked, we watched the morning sun cast a gorgeous golden glow over our little marina. Titus dropped rocks over the boardwalk railing and watched their ripples extend outward until the water was smooth again. We had only been out a few minutes when Titus pointed at the glassy morning water and said, "Look, Mama, peace." As I followed his gaze, I readily agreed. It's hard to find a more peaceful setting than the one that was before us.

The children and I had recently read a book about the fruits of the Spirit. I tried explaining that love, joy, peace, and patience weren't actual fruits to eat, but rather they were examples of what happens when you love Jesus and try to obey Him. Peace is hard to explain, but I tried. "It's that feeling in your heart when you want to take a deep breath and keep looking at whatever it is you see because it makes you feel calm." Yes, Titus, this was a perfect example of peace.

We live in a world with very little peace. Watch the news and people are fighting all across the globe. Get caught in traffic and watch the road rage. Or better yet, just look around your own home. Chaos abounds—dirty dishes, toys, diapers, and oh, the ever-growing pile of laundry! It's anything but peaceful. In fact, it can often feel overwhelming.

There are storms of chaos everywhere. But the storms that get me are the storms in my own heart and mind. They are the uncertainties and the unpredictables in life. Financial worries, parenting woes, debilitating fatigue, and the ups and downs of marriage can all create an inner storm of turmoil. These storms have the ability to discourage and easily become all-encompassing worries.

The good news is that Jesus has promised us peace. In fact, one of His names is even the Prince of Peace. After Jesus and His disciples had finished their Passover meal, Jesus shared basically His last big sermon to these core followers. Jesus knew His time was short, and this would be His very last time to teach them before He was to die. He chose a message of gentleness and promise in John chapters 14–16. His words of peace have the power to bring so much comfort. He said, "Peace I leave with you; my peace I give you…I have told you these things, so that in me you may have peace. In this world you will have trouble. But take heart! I have overcome the world" (John 14:27; 16:33).

Did you see what Jesus snuck in there? He said we will have trouble in life. It's inevitable. You can't escape it. And you know, my trouble will look different from yours. We all live different lives with our own circumstances and experiences. But we all have the same Prince of Peace who has given us His peace. When we take our storms to Him in prayer with thanksgiving, we are promised a peace that transcends all understanding to guard our hearts and minds in Christ Jesus (Philippians 4:7). That is powerful. So no matter what storm surrounds, you can have peace. The deep, cleansing breath of calm.

Do you need to experience God's peace? The kind that doesn't make sense? The kind that guards your heart? Guards your mind? The peace that is unexplainable? The inner calm like the glassy sea? It comes from relying on Christ and giving Him your storm. Give Him today, the worries, the chaos, the relational stress and let His peace guard and protect your mind.

Jesus, there is so much chaos in my life right now. There are things I'm holding that are making a storm in my mind. Thank You for all You promise and please bring the peace to my heart and mind that You said You will bring. Thank You for being the Prince of Peace. Amen.

55

Comfort and Joy

—— *Suzanne* ——

I couldn't believe what was happening. Five days before Josiah's second birthday, he had been admitted to the hospital with another potentially serious childhood illness. It hardly seemed fair, since the little guy just seemed to be getting back on his feet (literally, as he had just taken his first steps a month earlier) after his epilepsy diagnosis. But on his birthday, when most kids would be enjoying cake and opening gifts, Josiah took an ambulance ride from our local hospital to the children's hospital in Denver. I have a video of him sitting in his hospital bed that night, a bright red rash covering his face and a balloon tied to the guardrail.

"How old are you, Buddy?" I ask.

"Doo!" he replies, holding up two fingers.

During the ordeal, I stayed with my in-laws, who lived 30 minutes from the hospital, so I could continue nursing my four-month-old, Sadie. Kevin camped out at the hospital with Josiah. The doctors were stumped by his symptoms, which they feared could indicate a serious or even life-threatening condition.

Finally, two days before Christmas, Josiah was diagnosed with an atypical presentation of a nonserious, treatable childhood illness. We headed home, exhausted. We had already canceled our holiday plans to travel to Washington to see my family, and I suddenly realized we hadn't even decorated our house for Christmas.

But when I turned the key to our townhouse and swung open the front door, I couldn't believe my eyes. A lit and decorated Christmas tree stood tall in the living room. Tears filled my eyes as I looked around and noticed our nativity scene, strands of white twinkle lights, and sentimental knick-knacks littering the surfaces of our little home and filling it with cheer.

I found out that some of the women from our church who worked with Kevin had come in that day and decorated our house for Christmas. They had coordinated with Kevin to bring in a tree, something we didn't have, and unpacked decorations they found in our storage closet. I can't put into words how their generous act encouraged my weary heart.

The first verse I remember memorizing as a child was Ephesians 4:32. I learned it in the King James Version, which says, "And be ye kind one to another, tenderhearted, forgiving one another, even as God for Christ's sake hath forgiven you." I know the second part of that verse is about forgiveness, but the first part is about kindness. God is kind. He is tenderhearted. And He often demonstrates His kindness through the generous acts of other people.

As Kevin and I gathered our little family back into our cozy home, now prepared for the day we celebrate God sending His Son to earth, we felt God's kindness to us, even in the midst of trials. We received more kindnesses during that time than I can recount from our families and friends, but that one stands out.

Think of a time someone cared for you or showed you kindness. How did you feel? Allowing others to care for you can be uncomfortable and humbling (especially when you are in the habit of caring for others). Those sweet ladies had to go into my basement and see the disarray of my storage closet to find those decorations (horrors!). I had to be "that mom" who hadn't decorated my house for Christmas halfway through December.

But my weakness was an opportunity for others to show me the kindness and tenderness of my heavenly Father. One of my favorite verses is 2 Corinthians 1:3-4, which says, "Praise be to the God and Father of our Lord Jesus Christ, the Father of compassion and the God of all comfort, who comforts us in all our troubles, so that we can comfort those in any trouble with the comfort we ourselves receive from God."

God, the Comforter, chooses to show us His kindness and comfort through other believers. Why? So that we will comfort others with the comfort we received. I love that! When I'm feeling like I don't have the strength or resources to reciprocate, that's okay. It's how this life with God is supposed to work. My turn to comfort someone else will come. And when it does, I'll be ready.

———————

Lord, thank You for Your presence and Your comfort.
Thank You for using other believers to show me Your
kindness and the love You have for me. When I'm going
through hard times, remind me that You will use my
experiences to comfort others. Show me today how I can
care for somebody who needs Your comfort. Amen.

56

Wisdom on a Roll

—— *Gretta* ——

C hristmas was fast approaching and our house was looking quite bare. Apart from the Christmas tree, we had very few decorations and even fewer funds to buy any. With three toddlers at home, two in diapers, our budget was tight. I don't mind not having things. A bit of a minimalist at heart, I don't get worked up about a lack of stuff. But I want the things I do have to be meaningful. And what could be more meaningful than Christmas decorations—each one a reminder of God Himself coming to dwell among us? Hallelujah!

But as I looked around the small living room with random toys strewn about the floor, I saw nothing tangible I could use to teach my children this incredible, real-life story. Frustrated, I asked God to give me wisdom. I needed a nativity scene—free, if possible. We had scraps of wood in the shed and all sorts of random craft supplies. So with my hot glue gun in hand, I set to work.

During naptime, I grabbed my husband's chop saw and cut the wood. Much to my surprise, I was able to eyeball the measurements for a stable. Then I hammered and glued it together. *Perfect!* Well, not as perfect as if a carpenter had made it—far from it. But it was perfect for my purposes.

Then came the real stroke of genius. I noticed some empty toilet paper rolls lying around the house and suddenly imagined them being Mary, Joseph, and shepherds. Over the next few weeks, as more rolls became empty, the kids and I decorated them with shapes cut from foam and other odds and ends. Each day we talked about more of the wonderful story of Jesus coming to earth. The cardboard faces were scribbled, and they had no arms or legs, but toilet paper rolls were perfect for chubby little hands.

During those sacred days, the story became real to us. And it cost me nothing but a little creative thinking. I have since purchased many other Christmas decorations. But every year, when the decorations come out, the toilet paper nativity is my favorite. And although my children are elementary and junior high age now, they still set it up and play with it as they retell the story.

In Colossians, Paul writes to a group of believers in the church. After his introduction, he dives right into praying for everyone. I love these words in Colossians 1:9: "We have not stopped praying for you… We ask God to give you complete knowledge of his will and to give you spiritual wisdom and understanding" (NLT).

While some parts of God's will can be hard to discern, I know without a doubt that His will for you and me is that we teach our children who He is. But sometimes that's hard. We need His help to be creative and make those stories come alive.

I find I'm constantly praying Paul's prayer for myself. "Give me wisdom, Lord. Give me spiritual understanding." My tendency when I read a verse like this is to think it only applies to huge decisions. And though God will certainly give me wisdom for the big stuff when I ask, He also cares about smaller, more daily decisions.

As odd as it may sound, I believe God showed me the empty toilet paper rolls around the house and gave me divine wisdom to turn them into Mary, Joseph, and the wise men. He did this so that I would be able to teach my children the very real story of Jesus becoming "God with us."

Where do you need God's wisdom and understanding today? Maybe you have a child who won't sleep at night or you need courage to begin potty training. Perhaps you're wondering how to answer your child's difficult questions. Take those frustrations to God today and ask for His wisdom to help you think outside your own box. Who knows? Maybe your own toilet paper rolls will become a teaching tool.

———————

Lord, I need Your wisdom. I know You've called me to be a mama and teach my children about You, but sometimes I don't know how to do that. Please bless me with creativity and a deeper understanding of how You are working in my family. Thank You that when I ask for help, You will always answer me. Please fill me with the knowledge of Your will today. Amen.

57

Growing Strong

—— *Suzanne* ——

My husband and I are not morning people. During our newly-wed days, this was fine. We could stay up late on the week-ends and sleep in however long we desired. Even now, being night owls allows us to have ample time together at night after the kids go to bed. Here's the downside: Sleeping in is a thing of the past.

On Saturday mornings (the only day we technically could sleep in), we have a hard time getting up. Because our older kids are past the point of needing immediate supervision in the morning, we will some-times allow them to go downstairs on their own to play or watch car-toons. I never really sleep when this happens. In my imagination, every rustle is them helping themselves to chocolate chips from the pantry; every clink is them rummaging through the knife drawer. When I can no longer handle the guilt of my babies fending for themselves, I drag myself out of bed.

One such morning I padded downstairs around eight after hearing some mysterious noises. I prepared for the worst, but as I rounded the corner into the kitchen, I saw my three oldest seated at the table, each with a bowl of cereal and a spoon. My five-year-old beamed. "Look, Mom! I poured everyone cereal *and* milk!" And the amazing thing was...*she had*. The milk jug had been under a quarter full, and she'd employed her older brother to reach the box of cereal and plastic bowls.

I could hardly believe it. Sadie was intoxicated by her success. And her siblings munched happily on their cereal. I guess I shouldn't have been so surprised. Gaining independence is a natural part of growing up. In fact, as mamas we *want* to train our kids to do things for themselves and experience the rewards of being self-sufficient. Even Jesus grew from a dependent child to a competent adult (Luke 2:52).

As fun as it is to see our children grow and master new skills, they are not the only ones growing. You and I are also on a trajectory of growth. Listen to Paul's words in Ephesians 4:14-15:

> Then we will no longer be infants, tossed back and forth by the waves, and blown here and there by every wind of teaching and by the cunning and craftiness of people in their deceitful scheming. Instead, speaking the truth in love, we will grow to become in every respect the mature body of him who is the head, that is, Christ.

When Jesus comes into our lives, we are baby Christians. Like children, we begin by learning the basics of the faith and then progressing to full spiritual maturity. As we read God's Word, practice the instructions within it, pray, spend time with mature believers, and sit under sound biblical teaching, we become more and more grounded and capable in the faith.

I find that encouraging. A year from now, I will not be where I am today. And five years from now, my faith will look totally different. Maybe I can't pour the cereal and milk right now, but in a little while, I'll be able to do it, no problem. The best part is, God has provided me with everything I need to grow. And as I master new tasks and become more firmly established in faith, my Father cheers me on.

Don't be afraid to grow, Mama. Push yourself out of your comfort zone. Dig into God's Word. Join a Bible study or go to a women's conference. Serve where you don't feel quite ready. Like Sadie, you might just stumble upon big success and surprise everyone, including yourself.

———————

Lord, thank You for setting me on a path for growth and giving me everything I need. Help my roots to go deep so that I can speak with truth and love and grow into full maturity. Give me courage to take on new challenges that push me out of my comfort zone and deepen my faith. Amen.

58

Arrows in the Quiver

—— *Gretta* ——

y father is number 5 of 8 children. Born in the '40s, his family wasn't the anomaly it would be today, but I think Grandma giving birth to all 8 children in only 12 years (!) was a bit abnormal even then. Of those 8, 6 had children of their own, of which I am number 13 of 24. And we 24 are doing our part to increase the human population too, with nearly 50 kids and counting among us. If we were to have a family reunion with just my dad's siblings and all their offspring, we could fill a small hotel! As the story goes (or how I always heard it), whenever my grandpa was asked why he wanted so many kids, he'd respond by saying, "Well, the world can always use another Hires." (And yes, that's Hires like the root beer, but that's a different story.) As a child I giggled at that response, but I was also proud to be part of such a wonderful family.

My grandpa died when I was pretty young, so I don't remember too much about him. But I do remember one year when we were all visiting his house, we decorated little sticks that were made into arrows and were then placed in a homemade quiver to display above the mantle in my grandparents' home. With it was the verse from Psalm 127:3-5: "Children are a heritage from the LORD, offspring a reward from him.

Like arrows in the hands of a warrior are children born in one's youth. Blessed is the man whose quiver is full of them."

Before having children I didn't really understand this verse. The one where children are compared to arrows. I thought it odd that kids would be used as a weapon. Sure, it made sense that children are a heritage or a blessing. And it definitely makes sense that children are a reward. I mean, I feel like I hit the jackpot when God made me a mom. But why are they to be arrows? And am I the warrior? The quick answer: Yes, as the parent I am the warrior, and they are arrows to fight against the evil in this world.

As mothers, we are the first people to teach our children what love looks like. Children learn in our home how to love Jesus. They learn about kindness, gentleness, working with others, and all the things necessary to be functioning members of society. And how, pray tell, do they learn these things? They will learn best when they see us loving Jesus. When they watch us display kindness and gentleness toward others, they learn how to be gracious and compassionate. As we step out in obedient faith, following God's lead, our children gain wisdom and courage to follow God too. You see, we are their first models of what it means to follow God. They are watching. They are learning. And as they learn, they strengthen as arrows.

One day these children will be adults in a world that desperately needs truth. A world that needs compassion. A world that above all needs Jesus. And in this world there is a constant battle for our hearts and minds. It's a huge battle, and one that won't end until Jesus returns. But in the meantime, God has asked—no, commissioned—us to be a part of it. Every time we stand for godly justice, we strengthen the arrow. Every time we offer forgiveness instead of hate, we aim straight. Every time we speak the truth even when it's difficult, we sharpen the point. And every time we share Jesus with others, we help in the battle for the lost. When we model godly living, our children pick up on it and are more prepared to one day do the same. That's why we are warriors. That's why our children are arrows.

Warriors train. They prepare. Warriors stand ready for what comes. As warrior moms, we must do the same. Train by pressing in to the feet of Jesus and learn from Him. Prepare by obeying God's call on your life as a mom, a wife, a friend. Stand ready by praying for your children as they grow and learn to love Jesus. It's the highest calling, and you have been commissioned for it. Your children are a reward. They are a heritage. And you are blessed to have them in your quiver. Your quiver will grow as your kids grow and build their own families. I don't know if my grandpa ever envisioned how big his family would become, but he was right. The world needs more people trained and brought up to love and honor God. Now, as the warrior that you are, strengthen, sharpen, and aim.

———————

Lord, help me rise to the calling as warrior. Help me teach my children to fly straight and strong. Remind me that as their first teacher, I have been called to show them who You are and how to follow You. Amen.

59

Missing the Point

—— *Suzanne* ——

W hen I first became a mom, I felt pretty good about the fact that I didn't compare myself to other moms. When it came to motherhood, I had resolved to "just do me," and I pretty much stuck with that when my kids were young.

I had heard about "mommy wars," where strong opinions about how to mother, or whether to stay home or go back to work, ignite tension between mommies. But I was determined to stay above the fray and see what kind of mom God had made me to be. I made it through the baby and toddler years with my oldest two mostly unscathed.

Then my oldest daughter started kindergarten.

Suddenly I noticed how much better other women seemed to be at "momming" than I was. I especially compared myself to the moms who were structured, an area I'm weak in. They seemed organized…confident…in control. I, on the other hand, was slapping together my son's PB&J (made with sunflower butter, of course) two minutes before he stepped onto the bus. Not to mention I frequently missed the memos on all the extras my kids could participate in at school ("You're supposed to have crazy hair today, *why?*").

That's when comparison kicked in. As the strengths of other moms shone, I became insecure about my own abilities. So naturally I tried to do more and perform better. I felt like I needed to prove myself in areas where I was coming up short. The thing was, I couldn't do it. I could only mother out of my own specific design—strengths and weaknesses included.

Paul may have known nothing of mommy wars, but he did have some things to say about comparison. At one point in his ministry, some rivals were trying to discredit him by stirring up criticism about how he conducted himself as a servant of Christ. Paul had something to say about his critics in 2 Corinthians 10:12: "But when they measure themselves by one another and compare themselves with one another, they are without understanding" (ESV). *The Message* paraphrases it: "But in all this comparing and grading and competing, they quite miss the point."

Wow. That's convicting. What is the point? This mom thing—my life—is not about me. It's about God and the work He is doing: in me, in my family, in my home, and ultimately in the world. Spending time comparing myself to others is counterproductive to God's purposes and gets in the way of me being the mom God created me to be.

At times my children will suffer because of my weaknesses, and I should always be seeking the Lord to refine me and make me a better mommy. But on the flip side, my children will be served by my strengths—my ability to really listen to them, my capacity to nurture their emotions and talk to them about God, my propensity for creative expression. In all things, I can trust that God is using me in very specific ways in my children's lives.

Paul goes on to say: "'If you want to claim credit, claim it for God.' What you say about yourself means nothing in God's work. It's what God says about you that makes the difference" (vv. 17-18 MSG).

While I may desire bragging rights for being an awesome mom, God's opinion of me is all that really matters. I don't have to have all the strengths others do; I need to be faithful with the ones He's given me. What about you, Mama? Are you ready to give up the comparing, grading, and competing? Let's do it together. And as we flourish in our own strengths as moms, let's claim the credit for God.

_____

Lord, thank You for calling me to the work of motherhood and specifically equipping me to raise my children and teach them about You. Your ways are amazing, and I give You the credit. Help me avoid the trap of comparison that limits who You designed me to be as a mom. Help me not to miss the point. I want to please You and gain Your approval in all that I do. Amen.

60

Holy in the Unexpected

———— Gretta ————

I often wonder how many mama hours I've logged in my car over the years. Second to my house, I spend the majority of minutes in my minivan. Laden with fishy crackers, spilled apple juice, toy cars, crayons, and lonely and lost socks, my van screams "small kids own this thing." We converted to a van once our third joined the family, and we've never looked back. It's a great vehicle. Big enough for the entire family, all the groceries, beach toys, and space for another friend or two. I love it.

But occasionally the car can make us all a little crazy. The inability to move around coupled with running errands and shopping has the potential to bring out the worst in us all. We've had some doozies of arguments and parenting struggles in that car, but nearly no other place offers such a perfect environment for the holy. It's in the car where we talk about the mean kid in preschool class. It's in this vehicle where some of the big questions of life have been asked and discussed. And it was here in my sacred minivan that I heard the question, "Mama, why did Jesus have to die on the cross?" It came out of nowhere. We were just driving home from town, and four-year-old Titus was thinking.

As we passed farms and houses and drove the road we see almost daily, I told him about our holy God. God longs for relationship with us, but because He is holy He cannot be around anything that is not completely perfect. I explained the problem of sin and its devastating effects on our relationship with God. God loves us, His creation, so much that He moved heaven and earth to make a way to commune with us. He sent Jesus, His perfect Son, to earth to pay the penalty for our sin, making it possible for us to draw near to God. It is in this sacrifice that our sin is wiped clean and we can stand before holy God. He sees us as spotless because of Jesus. When we acknowledge our sin and need for Jesus, then we can walk with God forever.

Mamas, let me tell you, my old, messy, smelly minivan had never looked more sacred and holy to me than it did in those minutes driving down the road. Titus became a Christ follower that day and asked Jesus to be his forever friend.

God speaks and moves our hearts in the most unexpected ways. Take Moses, for example. In the middle of his daily grind as he was tending his father-in-law's sheep, God revealed Himself through a burning bush. As Moses approached the bush, "God called to him from within the bush, 'Moses! Moses!' And Moses said, 'Here I am.' 'Do not come any closer,' God said. 'Take off your sandals, for the place where you are standing is holy ground'" (Exodus 3:4-5). God then told Moses a bit of His resume—who He is and what He has done—and then God commissioned Moses to do the impossible task of leading the Hebrew people to freedom. Moses certainly didn't see it coming. In fact, he argued with God for a bit about whether he could actually do what God was asking. But in the end, Moses obeyed God and led God's people to freedom.

God uses the ordinary for His holy purposes. He used the bush in the wilderness with Moses. He used my minivan on the country road for Titus. Believe me, your car is more than a tool to get from point A to point B. It is holy ground for God to do the miraculous. Look for what God is doing.

Have you given your life to Jesus? If not, would you like to? He's right there beside you, calling you to Himself. You only need to recognize your need for Him and believe that Jesus, God's Son, has paid the price for your sin. You surrender your will to God's and ask Him to be in control of your life. And now get ready for God to do the miraculous in you.

God will choose any method He wants to get your attention and draw you to Himself. Be ready and look for it. And maybe, just maybe, you will sing His praises as you journey down the road after seeing the miraculous and holy. Your children will ask difficult life questions. You will teach the lessons of godly character. But buckle up and take off your shoes, for you are standing (or sitting—or driving!) on holy ground.

———————

God, thank You for accepting me as Your child and for calling me to a purpose that is not my own. Help me see You in what I have always thought of as ordinary and to look for the miraculous there. Give me the tools to be ready for what You have in store, no matter what. Amen.

61

Living Lovable

—— *Suzanne* ——

My three-year-old, Amelia, sat on the lid of the toilet with her arms crossed. "Nobody thinks I'm lovable," she said with a pout. "People think Jo is lovable and Sadie is lovable, but nobody thinks *I'm* lovable."

Our morning had been hurried, and many of my interactions with my middle child had been sharp. After one-too-many rebukes, her little heart could handle no more. She ran into my bathroom and shut the door. That's when I heard her murmuring her sad conclusion: *"Nobody thinks I'm lovable."*

I called her out of the bathroom, knelt down, and gave her a hug. Then I looked her in the eye. "That's not true," I said. "*I* think you're lovable."

Those words were all she needed to hear. She smiled with satisfaction and ran off to play.

Our interaction reminded me of the question that lingers deep within my own soul: *Am I lovable?* I'm a people pleaser, so it's a question I've spent a fair amount of time thinking about. It played through my mind growing up as I sought to make choices that would please my parents and win their approval. It plagued me as a 20-something who wanted to be married but spent many Saturday nights home alone. I silently ask it each time I look to my husband for affirmation and affection. And it whispers in my heart as I parent these precious little ones, knowing I'm making far too many mistakes.

At times I feel very unlovely and wonder, *Am I lovable?* The wonderful truth is that Scripture offers a definitive answer to that question: yes! Though I was unlovable by nature—born in sin—God loved me. Most of us are familiar with John 3:16, which says, "God so loved the world." I don't know about you, but I often picture a classroom globe when I hear that verse. But Ephesians 5:1 makes it personal when it says, "Follow God's example, therefore, as dearly loved children." Other versions translate that those words "as beloved children."

As a parent, I understand the concept of beloved children. My devotion to my kids runs deep, and at times I feel my heart will burst from how much I love them. The unbelievable truth is that is how God feels about you and me! To say that you are lovable would be an understatement. You are *dearly* loved. You are *beloved.* God thinks about you. He feels pride over your successes. He delights in the relationship you share. Based on your position as a child of God, you never have to question your lovability.

Ephesians tells us how dearly loved children respond: They follow their Father's example. They act like Him. Ephesians 5:2 gives further instructions: "And walk in the way of love, just as Christ loved us and gave himself up for us as a fragrant offering and sacrifice to God." Lovable children walk in love. Instead of being crippled by insecurity or self-doubt—locking themselves in the bathroom and crossing their arms—they radiate God's love to those around them. The love they feel from the Father overflows and spills out on everyone around them.

Mama, you are dearly loved. If you are feeling unlovable today, lift your eyes to your Father, who says, "*I* think you're lovable." And you can trust that He means it; He sent His Son to prove it. Maybe, like my daughter, that's all you really need to hear today.

Lord, thank You for loving me. When I'm feeling unlovable, remind me that I am dearly loved by You. Help me love like You do. Overwhelm my insecurities and doubts about myself with the truth about Your love for me. Help me love extravagantly the way You do. Amen.

62

Way, Way More
Than You Know

—— *Gretta* ——

I have a favorite children's book. Yes, after years and years of reading to the kids and many hours spent reading the same books over and over, I officially have a favorite. The book is not so much a story as it is a conversation between a parent and a child. In *I Love You So...* by Marianne Richmond, the parent expresses how much they love the child and the child continually asks questions, trying to define this love. Questions like "When I'm sick? When I'm messy? When I don't obey? And the parent continually answers each question with great tenderness and constant affirmation of their love for their child. The book begins and ends with this most fantastic dialogue:

"I love you."

"How much?"

"So much."

"How much is so?"

"Way, way more than you know."

This book is delightful, and I love reading it to my children. It didn't take us long to adopt the language ourselves and share in the same conversations. The best, though, was with Koen when he was still learning to talk. He'd sometimes start the conversation: "Mama, wuv you."

"How much, Koen?" I replied, eager to play the game with him.

He'd sing his answer, "Way mo no no!"

I know, cute, right?

Over the years we've had variations on this conversation. But this one I remember completely.

"I love you to the moon."

"Really, Koen? Well, I love you to the moon and *back*!" I responded.

Then, after thinking a bit, Koen replied, "I love you to the moon and to Jupiter and back. Then again and back. To Mexico, to England and back. I love you the most." (Oh, my heart.) He had imagined the farthest away places he could think of in order to express the most love he could possibly hold.

But I found myself repeating what my own wise father used to say when I was a kid. "Buddy, that's an awful lot, but you can't actually out-love me. I will always love you more. Because I'm your mama." He almost looked sad at the thought that he couldn't love me more, so I explained. "Koen, I'm your mama. I gave birth to you, and I know you. I take care of you, and I love you more than you can possibly understand right now. I know you love me as much as you can, but as your mama, I will just love you more." He seemed to be okay with that, though we have come back to this delightful discourse many times since.

It's true. There is a different kind of love that a mom gives her child. I want to see Koen grow and learn. I enjoy watching his character develop. I support him and encourage him. I'm there when he needs to cry. I take care of him when he is hurt. I feed him. I make sure he has clothes to wear and a comfortable place to sleep. I *know* my son, and I will do whatever it takes to help him grow into the man God wants him to be. Yes, Koen loves me too. But not remotely in the same way.

I can't help but see the imagery here between me as a parent and God as my heavenly Father. His love for me, for you, is absolutely immeasurable. We can try to understand, but we will never out-love God. He created us. He is eager to watch us grow and learn. He provides for our immediate needs. And, friend, He moved heaven and earth to have a relationship with us. He gave His Son (John 3:16), and the Son willingly endured hell so we can be forgiven and free. "See what great love the Father has lavished on us, that we should be called children of God! And that is what we are!" (1 John 3:1). Admittedly, there are times I question God, just like the child in the book I love so much. "Really, God? Even when I don't obey? When I hurt others? When no one else loves me? Do *You* still love me?" And beautifully and unfathomably He tells us, "I have loved you with an everlasting love; I have drawn you with unfailing kindness" (Jeremiah 31:3). And just like Koen, I can't fully understand, but I accept it to the best of my ability.

Mama, do you need this today? Are you questioning like a child? His love doesn't change, and you will never out-love Him. It doesn't depend on how you feel about Him and you can't do anything to earn it either. So, as a child, you can function and thrive in the security of His everlasting love.

———————

God, wow, wow, wow! Thank You for loving me. Sometimes
I question Your love because I just can't understand how
You do it. But help me understand, just like I want my own
children to understand how massive Your love truly is. Amen.

63

A House United

—— *Suzanne* ——

I'll never forget Kevin's and my most disastrous date of all time. It was our first date after the birth of our third child. I was an exhausted ball of hormones and had tried on three outfits before deciding on maternity jeans and an oversized blouse. I wasn't feeling the best about myself, but I desperately wanted to connect with my husband.

The fight broke out as we were pulling out of our driveway. I asked him where he wanted to eat dinner and he said, "I don't care."

His less-than-enthusiastic response sent me into attack mode. "You don't seem like you even want to go on a date!" I said.

"I'm just tired," he admitted, adding fuel to my fire (because how dare the father of a newborn be *tired*).

Our argument continued in the restaurant, where my tears eventually scared our server to the point that he quit coming back to check on us. Kevin finally had to take our bill to the front desk to pay.

On the way home, we unleashed more hurtful words—I needed more support; he needed more affection. Both of us felt frustrated. Neither of us felt loved. I wish I could say the fight was over that night, but it took us a few days to pick up all the pieces, and honestly, a few months to repair all the damage we'd done.

I'm thankful our kids weren't old enough to be aware of our bad behavior that night. They are now. Recently I raised my voice a bit as I was passionately trying to make a point to Kevin, and our three-year-old knit her eyebrows and said, "Are you guys fighting?" I was glad I could tell her that we *were not*, but little did she know how far Mommy and Daddy had come since that fight just after her birth.

Somewhere along the line, Kevin and I realized that there was a spiritual battle going on for our marriage. Over and over again in Scripture, God talks about unity. It's a trademark of the Christian faith that is modeled in a specific way between husbands and wives. They are to be "one flesh" (Genesis 2:24). And in our home, Satan seemed to be executing a full-court press to disrupt that unity.

This may seem like a marriage thing more than a mom thing, but the two are closely related. Unity with your spouse is the foundation of the house you're building for your children. In the Gospels, Jesus said, "If a house is divided against itself, that house cannot stand" (Mark 3:25).

I'm happy to say that through wise counsel, prayer, and intentional communication, Kevin and I were able to find more healthy ways to work through heated emotions. I'm glad, because my daughter's recent response to even minor discord between her parents highlights how much our unity matters to our kids. Our oneness provides them with a sense of security and refuge.

While there are certainly big divisions that can come into a marriage, the vast majority of divisions I've observed are small and come on slowly. When Kevin and I had our disastrous date, feelings exploded that had been on a slow simmer for weeks.

We had to learn to confront minor divisions immediately and recognize them as attacks from the enemy. If you are married, how are you doing in the unity department with your spouse? If you've let minor divisions build up in your relationship, it's time to mend them. God wants oneness for you and your spouse so that it can overflow into your home.

Lord, I can get so wrapped up in being a mom that I
forget the importance of being a wife. Help me to be on

guard against divisions creeping into my marriage. I pray that You would help us build a strong, unified home for our children. Thank You for Your wonderful plan for our marriage and family. Protect us from forces that divide and show us how to be united in You. Amen.

64

Mirror Messages

———— Gretta ————

There was a time in my life when I was great with regular devotions. I read my Bible daily, journaled regularly, and participated in a women's Bible study that not only met weekly but required nearly an hour of daily homework just to keep up. It was great. I loved the constant spiritual challenge and growth. And then Kaia came into the world, followed by Titus a year and a half later, and Koen in another 15 months. Before I knew it, I had lived a good four years without feeling like I had spent any quality time with God. I was living on fumes and often felt depleted spiritually. That is, until I remembered a trick Suzanne and I did in college—the art of writing on the mirror.

I don't remember who started it, but we would write verses on the mirror in our dorm room. We wrote with lip liner, eyebrow pencil, and then finally the much cheaper, dry-erase marker. We put up messages of encouragement and verses to remind us of God's faithfulness. We read them so much that some of the verses even were committed to memory.

So I looked around and realized a number of things were happening to me.

1. I had very small children.

2. These children would never leave me alone. (I mean, I only

got to shower if they were [a] in the tub with me or [b] in their beds asleep.

3. My brain had morphed into this new, foggy "mama brain" and I couldn't read deep, long, life-changing words.

4. I wanted to sleep every chance I got.

All this meant I needed to modify my time with God. Really, I needed to change the expectation I had on myself and what it meant to be a woman of God in this season. I did two things right away. First, I picked up a verse and wrote it on an index card and put it on my kitchen cupboard. Second, I started dance parties with my littles.

These parties became so life-giving I couldn't believe it. We'd crank worship songs and make up our own silly actions and dance routines. Sometimes the songs were lively, and sometimes they were more contemplative. But always, they pointed our thoughts to Jesus.

Slowly the atmosphere in our home changed because we were spending time daily in the Word. The verses on the cupboard lasted until they were memorized, and that simply happened because I read them so. Many. Times. I still know the dance moves to many of our favorite worship songs and now can embarrass the kids when we sing them in church. (Bonus!) It's the lesson that just keeps on giving so many years later.

When Moses was prepping the Israelites for life in the promised land, he gave them many encouragements for how to live. He reminded the people about the commands from the Lord for living well.

Deuteronomy 6:5-9 says,

> Love the LORD your God with all your heart and with all your souls and with all your strength. These commandments that I give you today are to be on your hearts…Tie them as symbols on your hands and bind them on your foreheads. Write them on the doorframes of your houses and on your gates.

So basically, tattoo God's Word all over the place so you see it and can't forget it! What better way to "bind it on your forehead" than to write verses on your mirror that will appear on your forehead as you brush your teeth in the morning! Get creative! Bible study *with* littles looks different than *before* littles. Have fun with it. If you'd like, you can even use the first verse I used just to get you started:

> So then, just as you received Christ Jesus as Lord, continue to live your lives in him, rooted and built up in him, strengthened in the faith as you were taught, and overflowing with thankfulness (Colossians 2:6-7).

It's a great verse! But there are thousands more to choose from. The only question left is, where will you put it?

God, help me understand that I can still have time with You even though it looks different now than it did before I became a mama. Give me Your creativity to study Your Word throughout the day. Amen.

65

Beauty in Imperfection

—— Suzanne ——

A few years ago on Labor Day, I decided we were in desperate need of a family fun day. Here's a law of nature: Make plans for a *fun* day with three young children, and you're just asking for trouble. But we had been working hard, and I'd made up my mind that we needed it.

The initial plan was to go out to breakfast and drive to our favorite little Colorado mountain town. But a quick check of the morning weather report told me it was cold and rainy in the mountains. Not a great environment for toddlers. So we shifted gears and decided to go to our favorite little diner for breakfast. We drove 40 minutes to where the foothills meet the mountains. But when we arrived, it was apparent from the crowd that we weren't going to get a table till lunchtime.

We decided to try another nearby breakfast spot, but we arrived to find the power had gone out and they weren't serving full breakfast. They were selling the donuts they had on hand...for cash. The $7 I dug out of my purse got us half a dozen donuts to tide us over. By this point, we were set on breakfast, so we drove back down to Colorado Springs to another favorite restaurant and sat down to our hard-won pancakes at 1:08 p.m.

Not the day I'd imagined.

When we got home, I made Kevin take a picture of the kids and me sitting on the front porch. I just needed *something* to prove we'd made a memory and had a good day. I needed evidence that our comedy of errors hadn't been a total wash.

Even though this event happened a few years ago, it could have happened last week. I've discovered that many days just don't go as planned. I intend to finish a whole to-do list and only check off one or two things. I look forward to a fun day with my kids and watch as my plans go off the rails (sometimes in dramatic fashion). My soul longs for completion, but everything feels incomplete.

In 1 Corinthians 13:9-10,12, Paul writes,

> We know in part and we prophesy in part, but when completeness comes, what is in part disappears…For now we see only a reflection as in a mirror; then we shall see face to face. Now I know in part; then I shall know fully, even as I am fully known.

This longing for completion isn't just a mom thing (although it may be intensified during this season of raising young children), it's a human thing. Our days here on earth are just part of the picture as our souls strive to put everything in order and do away with all the question marks. My desire for that perfect photo (which was a feat to accomplish in and of itself) was evidence of a deeper need—a need to find the perfection of all things in my Savior.

What hope and peace it brings me to know that one glorious day, everything will become clear and I will be fully known. Each insecurity and flaw will dissolve in a floodlight of truth. The incomplete will be made complete. Soak that in, Mama. One day nothing will stand in the way of a "perfect day."

Until then, I'm learning that flexibility has its charms. That day that fell far short of my expectations wasn't a fail. We spent time together as a family. We enjoyed the beauty of the day as we drove from place to place. We even arrived home in time for a nap, allowing the holiday to end on a relaxing note. When plans change, sometimes I'm pleasantly surprised by what happens instead. That's part of what makes life sweet.

————————

Lord, thank You for placing longings in my heart that point me to You. Thank You that one day You will make all things perfect and complete. Until then, help me see the beauty in the imperfection and the sweetness in the incomplete. Open my eyes to the many ways You're working in my unfinished places each day. Amen.

66

A Few Prickles

—— *Gretta* ——

Kaia was four and came running to tell me Koen had fallen down and was hurt. I didn't see him, but I heard the cries. We were at a playground we visited daily, and I was talking with another mom and didn't see what happened. Kaia told me he fell off one of the platforms, but she didn't think he was too badly hurt. Koen's cries told me a different story. He was only 18 months old, and I could tell he was in pain. I scooped him up and checked over his body, but he kept holding out his favorite sucking thumb and wouldn't let me touch it. In fact, he screamed when I'd go near it. It's hard when a toddler who can't speak gets hurt, especially when you didn't see it happen. But Koen was consistent: Normally when he was really sad, he'd suck his thumb and all would be somewhat better. But he couldn't even console himself because his thumb was the problem.

I dropped Kaia and Titus with a friend and took Koen to the ER to get his thumb checked out, fully expecting to get X-rays and leave with my toddler in a cast. His cries subsided as we sat waiting for our turn. The longer I sat, the more I wondered if I had made the right decision to bring Koen to the emergency room. His thumb wasn't swelling, and he occasionally let me touch it. But since we had come this far, we stayed.

By the time they called us back, his tears had dried and he seemed pretty okay. I held him on my lap while the kind doctor gently manipulated Koen's thumb. I couldn't see anything wrong, but the doctor was thorough and pulled out his big microscope with the bright light and found about ten iridescent prickles embedded in Koen's right thumb. With gentle precision he pulled each pointy thorn out of Koen's thumb, and as soon as the last one was removed, Koen plopped his fat finger happily back into his mouth as though he had never been wounded in the first place. I felt simultaneously silly and grateful. The doctor did what I could not.

I sometimes feel like Koen. I need help, I'm in pain, and I just need a doctor to heal my hurting heart. I've had arguments with my husband that have left me wounded. I have felt like a failure as a mother, wondering if I have ruined my children because of my mistakes. I have struggled with feeling "less than" and battled inner dialogue that would shock and dismay most people. But I take great comfort in knowing the world's best doctor who can help. Psalm 147:3 says, "He heals the brokenhearted and binds up their wounds." God is a doctor who is in the business of healing hearts. The psalmist who writes these words sings songs of praise to God, the One who delivers, who sees, and who heals.

He heals the brokenhearted. It doesn't matter how the breaking happened, God can heal. That's because he is Yahweh Rapha, the Lord who Heals. Sometimes our hearts break. They break because of wounded relationships. They break because of unfulfilled dreams. They break because of sin. They break because of unmet expectations. Our hearts break.

Where are you broken right now? What hurts? Let me offer you hope and encouragement. Because God is in the healing business. I don't know why you are experiencing the pain you feel; I wasn't there to see it. But even if you can't fully express what happened, you *can* take your hurt to the Doctor, the Healer, who will put your wound under His microscope and remove the prickles that no one else can see. He's the professional. Trust Him.

———————

God, thank You for understanding the pain and hurt inside my heart. I come to You, the healer, with my brokenness, knowing You are the only one who can truly see what's going on and can heal it. Amen.

67

The Art of Accepting Help

———— *Suzanne* ————

Thanksgiving was just around the corner when we learned we would be moving from Colorado to California for my husband's new job. We would have to act quickly to sell our house and move by the first of the year. While Kevin was wrapping up loose ends at his current job, I struggled to manage the household duties with a five-, three-, and one-year-old at home.

I didn't want to inconvenience anyone, so at first I did my best to "handle" it on my own. *I can do this,* I told myself. *I'll pack while my son is at preschool and the baby naps—no problem.* But it was a problem. When my own efforts weren't doing the trick, I finally reached out to a few close friends and Kevin's parents, who gladly came and helped me pack.

But even with that help, I was falling behind. And I was becoming increasingly uncomfortable asking for help. I felt I was asking for more than my share. In my estimation, my neediness was nearing an unreasonable level.

Everything came to a head the day I had to stage the house for the Realtor's photos. Kevin was tied up at work, and at the last minute, I reached out to a friend to come bail me out. She was working that day and arrived almost an hour later than planned. By that time I was frazzled and tearful and in the midst of a mad battle to keep my toddlers from undoing everything I'd done.

Janelle gave me a long hug and said, "It's okay." Then she jumped in, going from room to room, scooping clutter into a laundry basket. By the time the Realtor arrived, we were able to make the place look nearly spotless...one room at a time. As the photographer moved through the house, I shuffled my littles and their pile of toys from room to room while Janelle perfected the room being photographed.

I was seriously grateful for my friend's help, but I was also embarrassed and a little ashamed. I know the Bible says that we're supposed to help one another. But, frankly, I don't like to be the one in need. I'd much rather be the helper. I don't like to *have to* depend on other people. Asking for help when you know you can reciprocate is one thing, but being truly indebted to someone is another.

And yet, I have experienced more humbling moments of need as a mom than in any other time of my life. There are times when I simply would not have made it without the help of a friend or my family. That's humbling...and beautiful.

We live in a world that celebrates self-sufficiency. My instinctual "you can do this" pep talk to myself demonstrates this mind-set. None of us wants to "be a bother" to others. But God used my neediness to remind me of His design. He purposely created the body of Christ with dependence, not independence, in mind.

Consider the words of Romans 12:4-5: "For just as each of us has one body with many members, and these members do not all have the same function, so in Christ we, though many, form one body, and each member belongs to all the others."

If we're honest, we're all needy in one way or another. And that's not a bad thing. It's how God planned it, so we'd have to live interdependently. It's okay to need help, Mama, and lots of it. When your friend offers to take your child to preschool or babysit for date night, say yes! If you're facing a day (or week) that feels completely overwhelming, invite someone to help you out. You are giving them an opportunity to be blessed as they serve you. And someday soon you'll get the chance to help—I guarantee it.

In the years since that humbling meltdown, I have desperately needed others to help me on multiple occasions. And I've learned its okay to let someone bail me out. It's more than okay; it's how God designed it.

Lord, thank You for the body of Christ. Thank You for designing it so I don't have to do everything on my own. When I'm overwhelmed or weak, show me how to ask for help and depend on others. I pray a special blessing on those who have "bailed me out." Continue to help me lean on others in this beautiful journey of motherhood. Amen.

68

God's Painting

——— *Gretta* ———

They still say it every fall morning when we get to the stop sign. "Wow, Mama. Look at God's painting today." This observation began very simply one day as I was trying to describe to the children why I loved foggy mornings. We live about 20 minutes from town, and the majority of the drive takes us through woods and countryside. When my daughter was in preschool, we'd take an especially picturesque route to drop her off at school at least twice a week. After winding through the woods for five minutes, the road Ts, and there, at a stop sign, the view really opens up. As the car would come to a stop, we would look out over a rolling farmer's field with a small lake at the bottom. The mountains in the distance, mostly covered with trees, hid the sun as it rose to welcome the new day.

The warmth of that sun would soon burn off the wispy fog that dotted the landscape. "It's so froggy out, Mama," my daughter would say. (I admit I still don't correct them on this one. "Froggy" in the Kennedy household translates to "foggy," and I love its cuteness too much to change it.) Every morning view was different, but it was always breathtaking. And I would imagine God sitting in heaven with a paintbrush creating these beautiful landscape pictures. Sometimes for His enjoyment and sometimes just to see my own delight in it.

That's when I began sharing this delight with my young children in the car on our way (often running late) to preschool. I would say, "Look at God's beautiful painting!" This led to us constantly looking for His creativity in nature. We would see an exceptional butterfly and comment on how God must have had fun with that one. Or we would talk about how He made the creek to sound like happy singing as it spilled over the rocks.

In those moments, I had to agree with David the songwriter when he wrote Psalm 14

> Praise the LORD from the heavens! Praise him from the skies!…Praise him, sun and moon! Praise him, all you twin-kling stars!…Praise him, vapors high above the clouds!…You…mountains and all hills, fruit trees and all cedars…young men and young women, old men and children. Let them all praise the name of the LORD. For his name is very great; his glory towers over the earth and heaven! (NLT).

For generations people have seen God's glory in everything He makes. And for good reason. It's *amazing*! One of our beautiful jobs as mamas is to teach our littles how to praise Him. It can really be as sim-ple as noticing God's "paintings" and thanking Him for their beauty. It won't take long for those observations to turn into a lifestyle of praise.

And let me tell you, when you make a conscious decision to notice God's glory everywhere you look, your focus will begin to shift off yourself and onto God. And when you do that, the mess and the clutter isn't quite so bothersome. Today, look for opportunities to notice God's glory and point it out to your children. Then praise Him for it together.

God, today I want to praise You. Open my eyes to see Your glory, because it is all around me. Right here. In Your creation. Help me make a habit of praise. I want to teach my children how wonderful You are and how to worship. Show me Your paintings today, God. Help me model praise to my children. Amen.

69

Loving 152

—— *Suzanne* ——

My daughter Amelia likes to say, "Mom, I love you 152!" Right now it's the biggest number her three-year-old brain can fathom.

I'll say, "I love you 252!"

She'll pause, wrinkle her forehead, and say, "I love you 152 and 52!"

Although 152 is the biggest number in my daughter's repertoire, I understand the meaning of her words: "I love you to the greatest extent I can possibly imagine!" And I couldn't love the sentiment, or the girl, more.

This makes me think about how I express my love to God. I love Him, but the greatest praise I can come up with falls so short. I am limited in how I communicate my love. And yet, miraculously, I am able to have a relationship with Him—to love the One who loved me first. In Psalm 8:4, David asks, "What is mankind that you are mindful of them, human beings that you care for them?"

The question makes a good point. In all of the vastness of the universe, God is mindful of me. Not only that, but He invites me to be part of His family! I find it incredible that I can have a relationship with Him and be His child. Though my expressions of love and praise may be primitive, God created me that way. He also created my love with the propensity to grow, both in amount and in maturity.

In Philippians 1:9-11, Paul writes,

> And this is my prayer: that your love may abound more
> and more in knowledge and depth of insight, so that you
> may be able to discern what is best and may be pure and
> blameless for the day of Christ, filled with the fruit of righ-
> teousness that comes through Jesus Christ—to the glory
> and praise of God.

Just as my daughter's understanding and depth of love will grow
as she matures, my love will grow and flourish as I gain knowledge of
who God is and insight into His character and plans. This love will take
over my life, informing every decision and action, bearing fruit and
bringing Him praise and glory. Though I may feel inadequate at times,
I shouldn't let that stop me from expressing my love. In fact, in those
moments, the Holy Spirit intercedes for me (Romans 8:26).

How do you express your love for God? Are you timid, feeling like
you don't know what to say? Don't let that hold you back. Think of the
woman who poured costly perfume on Jesus' feet. She lavished Him
with her love, and He commended her actions.

My children have a front-row seat to watch how I love God. And
I can include them in my growing love for Him by going public with
my praise. While riding in the car, I can say, "Don't you just love God?
I do. I love Him because He is good! What is a reason you love Him?"
As they witness my clumsy attempts at loving God, they will feel more
comfortable to make their own.

Not long ago, I heard Amelia say, "I love God 152!" I smiled, happy
that her little heart is so full of love, for me *and* for the One who created her. I'm pretty sure her heavenly Father was smiling too.

———————

*Lord, I love You. Forgive me for the times I've been
timid about expressing my devotion to You. Thank
You for accepting my imperfect love. Help my love
to grow more and more and influence my children,
who are watching me. I pray that they would learn
to love You with their whole hearts. Amen.*

70

Dance Like Nobody's Watching

—— *Gretta* ——

When my youngest turned about two years old, he suddenly became aware that people thought he was cute. And really, he was cute. His smile could light up a room with his big eyes, even bigger eyelashes, and a dimple on his right cheek. Whenever someone outside our family squealed with delight at his cute face, Koen would grunt and look down at the ground, becoming fully aware of the fact that he was being watched. He didn't like being noticed. He didn't want to stand out, and he certainly hated to hear, "Oh he's so cute!" In fact, once he could talk at age three he turned to me one day and said, "Mama, why they say I cute? I not cute. I Koen!" Poor kid. It's hard to not stand out when your face shines.

My husband's job as a director at a kids' camp meant we spent a lot of time hanging out on the property during the summer. It was a great environment for our kids, but since it was a large camp, all the 150-plus summer staff knew who my children were even when my kids didn't know them. On the first night of each camp, the campers would head over to our chapel tent after dinner to get acquainted with the ins and outs of camp life for the week. The time always started with a live band playing music to get all the kids over to the tent. There is a huge field separating the dining hall from the chapel, and the music could be heard all the way across it. As we walked the field every week to listen to the music before heading home for bedtime, Koen would stop dead in his tracks, put his arms out to the side, and bounce. He couldn't continue walking if the music had already begun. And he'd stay there bouncing, until either the music stopped or I picked him up and carried him the rest of the way. There was just something about the music that made him dance.

And it didn't stop there. If we were under the tent, he made his way to a very specific spot on the floor to continue his "dancing." In those moments he didn't care that every person who could see him was enamored by his cuteness. He was moved by the music, and for once in his life he didn't care what everyone else thought. He just had to express himself.

I have to admit that sometimes I feel like Koen. I don't want to be noticed. I don't want people looking at me and making their own judgment calls about how cute (or not) I am. I can feel like I'm under a microscope when people learn that I am a Christian and they think they may judge everything I do or say. But then I remember King David.

David was king over all of Israel. During his reign, David sought to return the ark of the covenant back to God's people. The ark was a great symbol of God's presence and glory and had been stolen during one of the battles. For 70 years it was not with the Israelites. David longed for God's chosen people to be able to worship in Jerusalem, with the ark. As his lifelong dream was being fulfilled and the ark was brought back into the city, "Wearing a linen ephod, David was dancing before the LORD with all his might" (2 Samuel 6:14). He danced with joy, abandoning dignity and position to rejoice before the Lord. As a king, David looked ridiculous and undignified. But David didn't care. He was overcome with joy, gratitude, and worship. He couldn't merely stand in the courtyard watching a dream unfold before his eyes. No, he chose to dance. And when he was judged for his actions, he responded by saying, "I will celebrate before the LORD. I will become even more undignified than this, and I will be humiliated in my own eyes" (2 Samuel 6:21-22). His worship was without limits, without reservations, and without care.

Wouldn't that be freeing? Not to care what others thought? To be so overcome with joy and gratitude that we worship God with complete abandon? Now that's freedom. Like Koen in the field and like David in the court. What do you say? How about putting some music on today and dancing around the living room in worship? Think of how much God has done and truly worship Him for it!

Lord, I'd love to not care what others think of me. I'd love to just be able to completely worship You as David did and rejoice in who You are. Give me courage when I'm with people who make me feel insecure to just love You and worship You anyway. Amen.

71

Blowing It Big-Time

—— *Suzanne* ——

I knew I'd blown it. In fact, in my five years of being a mom, I'd never blown it worse.

Our minivan had rolled into the hotel parking lot somewhere in Montana after midnight. We were in the midst of a cross-country road trip, with three children five and under, to see my parents. Our 18-month-old had gotten car sick during the final leg of that day's journey, so after we had checked in, Kevin immediately headed to the laundry room to wash the soiled car seat.

As I attempted to calm our three littles and get them to sleep in unfamiliar beds, Josiah, who was five, jumped on the bed, thudding into the wall repeatedly. I kept telling him to get down, but he was working out energy reserves from a day stuck in the car.

When he bonked his head on the headboard and began wailing, I'd had enough. "Josiah," I whisper-yelled, roughly pulling him away from the bed. "Bad decision! That was a bad choice!"

My son immediately reacted to my anger. "Bad decision!" he said, hitting his head with his hands. "Bad choice!" He did it again before I was able to hustle him into the bathroom, where I set him down on the toilet seat cover and tried to calm him. We were both crying at this point. And I felt terrible.

This wasn't the first or last time I "lost it" with my kids, but it was a memorable one. As I watched the very obvious way my son, who has special needs, was affected by my anger, I vowed that it would never happen again.

Mom guilt takes many forms. Sometimes I feel like I'm not giving my children all the right experiences to thrive. Other times I can obsess over feeding them the right foods or whether I'm being a consistent role model. And then there are the times when the guilt is so, so real because I've obviously blown it.

We all blow it at times, and our failure does not surprise God. Scripture offers this very real hope in Proverbs 24:16: "For though the righteous fall seven times, they rise again, but the wicked stumble when calamity strikes." The righteous *will* fall repeatedly…but they will rise again. How amazing. And 1 John 1:9 says, "If we confess our sins, he is faithful and just and will forgive us our sins and purify us from all unrighteousness."

I don't know about you, but I am an imperfect mama. And I come from a long line of imperfect mamas. One of my most vivid memories from childhood is of my own mother coming into my room after she'd yelled at me and hurt my feelings.

"I'm sorry," she would say. "Mommy shouldn't have gotten so angry. I'm sorry for what I said. Will you forgive me?" I was always more than willing to forgive, but what really stood out to me was how my mom admitted that she needed Jesus too. When I made mistakes and hurt people, I followed her example of asking God to forgive me and then making things right with those I'd hurt.

As my son's distress mellowed into calm sniffles, I told him, "I'm sorry, buddy. Mommy shouldn't have yelled at you. Will you forgive me?" He stared at me with wide, trusting eyes and wrapped his arms around my neck for a snotty hug. My guilt didn't immediately go away, but I went to bed thankful that I belong to a God who always forgives and that He's created my children to be forgiving too.

Lord, I thank You that You forgive me when I confess my sin.
Thank You for new mercies when I blow it as a mom.

I praise You that I no longer carry the weight of guilt and shame because of what Jesus did on the cross. Help me proclaim that to my children through my life. I pray that they would experience Your forgiveness the way I have. Amen.

72

Comparison Versus Completeness

———— Gretta ————

For today's devotion I want to switch up the format and start off with a Bible story.

After the nation of Israel took over the promised land and Joshua died, they lived for several years establishing themselves as a nation. But after a little while they looked at the nations around them and noticed a difference...the nations all had a king. Israel began to get insecure and question their legitimacy. So they spoke to Samuel about it. "You are old, and your sons do not walk in your ways; now appoint a king to lead us, such as all the other nations have" (1 Samuel 8:5). Samuel disagreed, but took the matter to God, who responded by saying, "It is not you they have rejected, but they have rejected me as their king. As they have done from the day I brought them up out of Egypt until this day, forsaking me and serving other gods, so they are doing to you" (vv. 7-8).

Whoa...when the Israelites looked around and did their comparison, they failed to see they had everything they needed and more with God as their king. They were blinded by their dissatisfaction, jealousy, insecurities. They lost sight of who they were as God's chosen people. Even after they were warned of all the trouble and heartache a king would bring to them, they still said, "No! We want a king over us. Then we will be like all the other nations" (vv. 19-20).

They forgot that they were already complete as a nation. They were never supposed to be like all the other nations. They were uniquely God's.

I can also fall into the same trap as the Israelites. Like the time my husband called me mid-morning after speaking with a more seasoned mom on the phone. During their conversation she was making dinner…at ten in the morning. Jay was calling to give me a great idea of how I could plan ahead so I wouldn't be so stressed. He was trying to be helpful, but I heard, "You'd be a better mom if you were more organized and planned ahead."

Or the time a friend of mine with two kids of her own invited me and a couple others with small kids to her home every week for adult connection while our kids played together. I looked forward to this weekly outing until one day two-year-old Kaia told me, "Mama, their house is fun. They have fun toys." All I heard was, "Your kids would be happier if you had better toys."

And then it happened again when, a few months after my youngest was born, I got together with a group of friends I hadn't seen in several years, one of whom had had baby number four near the time of mine. We really had a fantastic visit, but in the back of my mind I kept looking at her much thinner body and thinking, *You'd be so much prettier if you would lose the baby weight like she did.*

I could go on and on with examples of how I have compared myself to others over the years. Every time I do it, I act just like the Israelites. I focus on my insecurities, and before I know it I become dissatisfied, jealous, and even more insecure. Comparison is pervasive, and if left unchecked, it can lead us down a path God never intended for us. You see, God made us complete in Him. Yes, we still need to grow and learn, but He designed us uniquely—us. And when we get caught up in comparing ourselves to others, not only do we spiral down into self-pity and inadequacy, but we unknowingly take God out of the king seat and look to find our own king. We play the "if only" game that never turns out well.

You and I were never meant to be like the ones we compare ourselves to. You are to be you—and only you—rooted and established in love, growing in the grace and knowledge of our Lord Jesus Christ, created in Him to do good works. If you and I were to just focus on those three things, we'd never have time to compare ourselves to others, and we wouldn't live in the jealousy and insecurity that comparison brings. Instead, we would recognize that we are made complete in Christ, lacking nothing.

We can learn from the mistakes of Israel. Next time you hear that voice in your head saying, "If only _____ (you fill in the blank)," grab that thought and toss it from your mind. Replace it with the truth of who God made you to be. Focus on your strengths, your gifts, and your talents. Then you will experience a peace that surpasses all understanding that will guard your heart and mind.

God, comparing myself to others is so easy to do! But I don't
want to be like Israel and be dissatisfied with how You
have made me and all the blessings I have. Please help me
focus on being complete in You instead, and on remaining
content with everything You have given me. Amen.

73

Post Office Blues

——— *Suzanne* ———

One morning, when Sadie was two and a half, I announced that we were going to the post office before we picked up her brother at preschool.

"I love the post office!" she shouted, clasping her hands together in excitement.

I was surprised by her response, because I'm pretty sure those words have never been uttered in the history of the world (at least not by a person who's waited her entire lunch break in line to mail a package). But I accepted her positivity as a small blessing and loaded her in the car for our adventure.

When we arrived at the "post office," which was actually one of those convenient little stores, Sadie kept looking around and saying, "Different place." A few times she tried to open the door that led to the back of the store, but it was locked.

When a fellow customer asked her how she was doing, Sadie gave her a puzzled look and said, "I came to a different place." The clerk behind the counter noticed Sadie's interest in opening the door and invited her back for a full tour. Even after that, Sadie seemed dissatisfied with her post office experience.

Back in the car, I asked her again, "Sadie, how did you like the post office?"

"I came to a different place," she replied, seeming rather disappointed. That's when it occurred to me that her only exposure to the post office was through a children's cartoon we had watched often. In the episode about the post office, letters and packages cheerfully sing and dance in their mail bins. In comparison to her expectations, the real post office was a huge letdown.

Have you ever felt like Sadie? You expected motherhood to be a little more magical and fun than the reality. Maybe you imagined having exciting adventures with your child, but meltdowns and tantrums are more the norm. Perhaps you find the work of motherhood overwhelming and unfulfilling, when you were sure you'd feel the opposite.

Instead of singing and dancing packages, you were met with a much less exciting reality. A friend once told me, "Where there are expectations, there will always be disappointment." We all have expectations about how our lives will go, and even what kinds of moms we'll be.

In high school and college, I was a sought-after babysitter who loved spending time with kids, so I expected I'd be a pretty great mom. I was shocked to discover how much I struggled with the daily tasks of being a mom, and (*gasp*) that I didn't enjoy it every single moment. At times the difference between my expectations and my reality created disappointment.

Proverbs 13:12 says this about human nature: "Hope deferred makes the heart sick, but a longing fulfilled is a tree of life." Many expectations for life begin as deferred hopes. And when those longings are fulfilled and the reality of it is different than we expected, disappointment can ensue.

I didn't meet my husband until I was 30, so I began to wonder if I would ever have the family I longed for. That may be why I feel so guilty whenever feelings of discontentment creep in. But the second half of that verse says, "A longing fulfilled is a tree of life." A tree is a living object that bears fruit over and over again. My children are a longing fulfilled, and God will use them to bring me life again and again throughout my days.

Does that mean every moment will be precious and magical? Nope.

There will be hard work involved and days of sorting plain letters into boring bins. There will also be heartache in letting go of some of the things I imagined. But as I focus on the reality of what God *has* done, I can gain new appreciation and joy for my circumstances, even if they're a little different than planned.

Had Sadie not pictured letters that sing and dance, she might have been more enthused by the calm, pleasant atmosphere, the friendly people, and the behind-the-scenes tour she received at the post office. As I learn to let go of my expectations and focus on how God has fulfilled my longings, I can see more fully the beauty of my reality.

———————

*Lord, thank You for fulfilling so many of my longings.
Help me let go of expectations and truly appreciate
my own, unique journey of motherhood. Help me
notice the many blessings around me today and gain
newfound joy in the things You have done. Amen.*

74

Stop and Look at Me

——— *Gretta* ———

I was fluttering around the kitchen making dinner, washing dishes, and putting away groceries. You know, managing my home. It's common to find me doing a little of this and a little of that while a million other thoughts run through my brain. It's constant. You know what I'm talking about. It's remembering doctor's appointments (stir the sauce). The phone rings—a solicitor again. Someone is whining in the other room (chop some cucumbers). Husband is home from work in 30 minutes. When was the last time I showered (stir the sauce again)? Is this how my mother did it? "Kids, just share the blocks." Oops, I didn't pull the meat from the freezer.

"Mama."

I should wash some plates so we can eat tonight. "Yes, Koen?" *Ding*, the microwave.

"Mama."

Go to the stove and stir again. "Yes, Koen. I'm listening." *Plunk. Plunk.* Someone is playing the piano.

"No, Mama. Stop. Look at me. See me."

Screech. I come to a full. Stop. I turn off the faucet. I bend down to his level and look in his eyes. For 20 seconds I see nothing else. I hear nothing else. Just my four-year-old's voice telling me something very important that was on his heart. He needed my whole attention to do it. It didn't take long. And he was right. I needed to stop. To look. To see him. I was multitasking like a mad woman, but there was so much in my head that there was no space for him. His four-year-old self knew my attention was all over the place, even though my 30-something self thought I could handle just one more thing. But he was right. I needed to be still.

We can get so wrapped up in our minds, our duties, our little worlds that we cannot hear God's voice speaking or even remember He is there. Just writing my thoughts and actions that were happening in the moment made my heart rate jump up a few beats per minute. It's no wonder God tells us to "be still, and know that I am God" (Psalm 46:10).

Can you just hear him? "Stop, Mama. Look at me. See me." This word, *still*, is translated in other parts of the Old Testament as "stop," "wait," "let go," "refrain." Take a deep breath—in—out. Do it now. In. Out. Be still. Quiet down. In His gentle voice, God calls you to stop. Have you ever wondered why? God knows that you're busy. He knows there are Cheerios on the floor. He knows you have everyone pulling on you. He also knows that when you wait, when you quiet your spirit, you can hear Him saying, "I got this." He's saying, "Trust Me. Know who I am and what I can do. Know—acknowledge and understand—I. Am. God."

So how can you remember to be still? Is it 30 seconds of deep breathing for you? Is it a note on your bedside table? For me, it's as simple as classical music while I'm folding laundry. It can be anything. But when you do find the moments of stillness, focus on God. Focus on His character. Focus on what He can do. And know, really know, He's got this.

Wow, God, I sure could use some stillness in my life. Give me the creativity to see where to be still in the middle of my crazy, wonderful life. Help me hear Your voice and trust that You are God…in all Your goodness and might. Amen.

75

Embarrassing Moments

Suzanne

One of my most embarrassing moments as a mom happened at camp. Our kids were four, two, and almost one when we packed up our minivan and drove to Sonrise Mountain Ranch in the Colorado mountains for a week of family camp. The combination of too little sleep the night before, seven hours of travel (including too many potty breaks to count), and rolling into camp as events were already underway left all of us feeling a little frazzled. We made it through dinner, but by the time we had gathered for worship in the lodge, Kevin and I had lost all control over our children.

As we sat in a circle for an unplugged, intimate worship time with half a dozen other families, Josiah, four, alternated running away from us and doing an exuberant interpretive dance in the middle of the circle. Following his cue, my two-year-old danced around the room, laughing impishly and evading our attempts to wrangle her back to our corner of the room. And the baby was, well…being a baby. Every so often she let us know (loudly) that she was ready for bed. There was nothing Kevin or I could do to get our unruly children under control.

That's when I felt tears brimming in my eyes. I was *so* embarrassed. I know I struggle with caring too much about what other people think.

But this was one of those moments where I really wished my children were a little less like themselves and a little more like the Von Trapps—lining up neatly and politely to impress the crowd with a good-night song.

I'm sure that at "family camp" those fellow parents completely understood what we were going through and weren't judging, but why did *my* children have to be the ones acting up? Josiah almost landed on a baby—not ours—during his interpretive dance, and during prayer, Sadie yelled, "I'm done!"—just in case there was any question.

Everyone was gracious to us following the debacle, but my pride was hurt. Even back at our cabin I couldn't stop the hot tears from flowing as I replayed "the incident" over and over again in my head. I felt like the worst parent ever.

I don't think anyone enjoys being embarrassed, but it's a part of life—especially life as a parent. Children can be embarrassing. I have to realize that my children are a work in progress. I was embarrassed because I believed that my rambunctious children were a reflection on my parenting.

Listen to the words of Psalm 62:7: "My salvation and my honor depend on God; he is my mighty rock, my refuge." Did you hear it? My salvation and honor depend on *God.* Not on my kids. And certainly not on my parenting abilities. Even better, Colossians 1:11 reminds us that when embarrassing moments strike, we can forge ahead, "being strengthened with all power, according to his glorious might, for all endurance and patience with joy" (ESV).

Later that night, as Kevin and I sat on the porch of our cabin, breathing in the fresh mountain air, we reviewed the facts:

1. We have a child with special needs.

2. We have a delightfully spirited, precocious, creative two-year-old.

3. We have a *baby.*

If that wasn't the perfect storm for some embarrassing moments, I don't know what is! I certainly have parenting flaws, but I also can't change who these precious little humans are…who God created them to be. If that bruises my pride, so what?

That day I needed to remember that my daughter wouldn't be two forever. Someday public interpretive dance would be a thing of the past. And when that happened, I would miss those embarrassing moments. At least some of them.

Until that day comes, I can soak in each moment of the process and allow God to strengthen me and give me joy…even in the awkward moments.

———————

Lord, sometimes my children embarrass me. You must understand that. Just as You give me grace when I'm headstrong and foolish, help me to be patient and gracious with my children. Help me take my eyes off of myself and realize that their childish exuberance is fleeting and You are with me in this task of raising little ones. Amen.

The Importance of Discipline

———— Gretta ————

E very spring my family attends a weekend family camp where my husband works. Our days consist of many exciting camp activities, games, sessions, and free time as a family. We hit the ground running from the time we wake up until our heads hit the pillow at night. The kids are constantly in motion running from one activity to the next, and really, they only stop long enough to eat something before they're off doing the next wonderful camp thing.

One year we were sleeping in a cabin, and I forgot to bring our bedtime reading material, which included the children's Bible. We try and make sure to read Scripture before bed every night, so I decided that in place of the Bible designed for little ones I would read from a grown-up Bible instead. The kids were snuggled in their sleeping bags on their bunks, and I read by the light of my headlamp as our cabin had no electricity. I picked up where I had been reading personally, which meant I read aloud from 1 Samuel 3.

This is the chapter where young Samuel hears the audible voice of God while he's sleeping and runs to his mentor and priest Eli, thinking Eli is calling. On his third visit during the night, Eli realizes God is speaking and he tells Samuel to answer God and listen to the message. So on the fourth time, Samuel answers God and God reveals to him judgment coming to Eli and his sons. To the sons for their willful disobedience, and to Eli for his unwillingness to discipline his sons.

It was silent in the dark as I read, and I was pretty sure the kids had fallen asleep to the sound of my reading voice trailing off. But I made my observations aloud anyway. For some reason, I'd never picked up on the message God had for Eli. I had only remembered the story to be about Samuel learning to recognize the sound of God's voice. But here, in the dark, it struck me that God was going to judge Eli for *not* disciplining his sons. And I said, "Wow, kids. I sure don't want to be like Eli. I want to always listen when God tells me I need to discipline you guys. See, I don't just discipline you because I'm disappointed or because I'm the mama. I discipline because I'm responsible to God for how I parent, and I need to obey God." Then, from somewhere in the dark I heard, "Whoa."

Yep, discipline is a big deal. And God takes it seriously. As parents, we discipline our children to teach them what is appropriate and so that as they grow they learn to be kind, respectful, responsible people. No one enjoys being around an adult who was never disciplined as a child and got everything they ever wanted. No, we love our kids too much *not* to discipline.

The same is true for God the Father. Proverbs 3:11-12 tells us, "My son, do not despise the LORD's discipline, and do not resent his rebuke, because the LORD disciplines those he loves." We, as adults, still make mistakes. We are selfish, defiant people who still need God's discipline in order to continue to grow into more of Christ's likeness. And that's the whole point, isn't it? To grow toward holiness. In fact, Hebrews 12:10-11 says, "God disciplines us for our good, in order that we may share in his holiness. No discipline seems pleasant at the time, but painful. Later on, however, it produces a harvest of righteousness and peace for those who have been trained by it."

The fact is, discipline hurts. It's uncomfortable, but it is designed to help us change our behavior. Discipline often looks like having to face the consequences of our bad decisions. Like when you hurt your marriage because you have hidden the truth from your husband and he finds out you've been lying to him. Or when you lose friends after they learn you've been sharing their secrets with others and you can't control your tongue. Or maybe you have been spending money you don't have and are looking at debt you can't afford to repay. I don't know where your sin has taken you, but I know God loves you, His child, too much to allow you to stay in it. He will discipline you as a good father should.

There is a reward to all this correction—a harvest of righteousness and peace. Oh, that blessed peace. The discipline is worth it. We know that for our kids, but do you know it to be true for you? Don't run from God's correction. It's for your growth and development as a woman of God.

———————

God, I don't like to face my sin. It's not fun. I'd rather hide it. But I know You see it all, and I trust that You are good and it's Your goodness that requires You to discipline me. Please help me set aside my pride and recognize that Your discipline is for my good and my growth. Help me learn through this process. Amen.

77

Nurturing Little Adventurers

———— Suzanne ————

When we first moved to California from Colorado, everything felt magical. Even checking out a new grocery store was exciting! Watching my kids splash in the Pacific Ocean for the first time will always be a highlight of my life. My oldest, in particular, could not get enough of the wind on his face or the movement of the waves that chased him. He got soaked, of course, but the look of pure joy on his face is something I will never forget.

During our first year in a new town, we explored all our new surroundings had to offer. We went to the farmer's market each weekend, selecting fresh oranges and strawberries and eggs. We drove two hours to a Christian camp in the mountains, where the kids marveled at giant sequoia trees. We visited LA and went to Disneyland. And we made it a priority to take a day trip to the coast at least every few months, exploring different beaches each time and even viewing an elephant seal rookery.

I can't really describe all the fun we had during that year of adventuring together. The town where we live is a family town in the central valley of California, and many people have lived here all their lives. So as we talked to new acquaintances, we discovered that in one year we had done things many of them had never done—or had done just on occasion.

And as I reflected on living in majestic Colorado when our children were very young, I realized that Kevin and I hadn't taken advantage of all the wonderful adventures right in our backyard. We liked to get out of the house and drive to the mountains occasionally, but we took it for granted. We had to move to get bitten by the adventure bug.

Exploring was good for our family, but it also reminded me of the innate desire for adventure God has put in our hearts. Following Him is not boring. As we read His alive and active Word, we can expect Him to do amazing things. And when we submit to Him, our path will be full of surprising twists and turns.

Listen to the words of Jesus in John 10:10: "The thief comes only to steal and kill and destroy; I have come that they may have life, and have it to the full." Other versions describe it as "living abundantly." That doesn't sound like sitting on the couch and going through the same old routine to me. Jesus calls us to the adventurous life!

Is your family getting enough adventure? A friend recently told me that they had taken their very first daytrip as a family with their young children. "It was really good for us," she said. "Our kids seemed to thrive on us having this special adventure together—just us."

Maybe you're new to your town or you've lived there all your life. Either way, don't forsake adventure. Don't be so practical that you miss out on living abundantly with your kids. Get out and explore the mountains or the city or the forest. Take advantage of your local parks, zoos, and aquariums. Not only will these experiences create lasting memories, they will also provide a taste of the kind of life Jesus offers— a grand adventure together.

Lord, thank You for offering me life to the full. I know I don't always live with awareness of that. I pray You would call my children to the abundant life only You can offer. Help me model the adventure of being Your follower. Show me opportunities to adventure with my family and introduce them to the big, exciting, meaningful life only You can give. Amen.

78

Just Add a Bit of Kindness

———— *Gretta* ————

A trip to McDonald's has always been a special outing for my kids. Living in a climate that is wet and rainy nine months of the year means we don't get to play outside at the park very often. So we find as many free indoor places to run, climb, and wiggle as possible, and McDonald's can always be trusted to provide such a place for us.

Koen was four years old, and while his older two siblings were at school, I decided to take him to the fast food joint. During that year I took care of a little two-year-old girl during the day and she joined us on our trip. Koen was great at looking out for her. He often held her hand to help and protect her when we were out.

We walked in together, and I asked Koen to take her to the playland area while I stood in line to order us some muffins. I watched as he took her hand and walked her to the other side of the store to play while they waited for me. There were a number of teens sitting in the booths watching him, and as he passed, they smiled and snickered among themselves.

When I joined the kids in the play place, he very sadly asked me, "Mama, why were those big kids laughing at me?" I responded, "What do you think was going through their minds, buddy?" Koen thought for a moment and replied, "They probably think a boy shouldn't hold a little girl. Maybe they think I'm too old for that. But, Mama, if I didn't hold her, how would she know where to go? I had to help her. I think they laughed because they didn't know. Sometimes people just don't know."

Wow, this little four-year-old has so much insight. Sometimes, actually often, people just don't know. They don't know (or remember) what it's like having tiny tornadoes in the house who destroy all the cleaning you've done. They don't know how hard it is to lose weight when all you have to eat is leftover cold mac and cheese and you're not sleeping for more than three hours at a time. They don't know that your trip to the grocery store is your big outing for the week and their judging looks as your baby cries through the checkout lane really aren't helping.

But you know, the same can be said for you. You don't know that the person who cut you off on the highway is dealing with some great heartache and isn't paying the best attention to the road. And you don't know that the friend who doesn't seem to be happy about all your baby's milestones just miscarried…again.

The truth is, none of us really knows what is going on in another's life. And apart from hearing everyone's story and circumstances, we can never be sure. It's for this reason Paul's words in Colossians 3:12 are so important for us to hear. "Therefore, as God's chosen people, holy and dearly loved, clothe yourselves with compassion, kindness, humility, gentleness and patience."

We know the importance of teaching our children to be kind and to think of others, but do we practice it ourselves? The reality is, it can be hard to be kind when we feel offended or wounded or when we are just plain unhappy with a particular situation. But you know, when we realize the depth of love we have received, when we understand that our standing with God is a result of nothing we have done to earn it but rather it's merely because we have been chosen to be His child, that is when we can turn and show kindness, compassion, humility, gentleness, and patience to everyone else. Because of Christ. Because of God's holiness. Because of love.

Now that's a good reason to be kind. In the words of Koen, "Sometimes they (and we) just don't know." But we are kind anyway. How can you practice this today? Who needs a bit more understanding from you? How can you humble yourself today and offer more kindness?

———————

Lord, help me remember that everyone has their own story and needs kindness. Give me the courage to be kind even when it's hard. As I understand more what You have done for me, help me treat others with the same generosity You have shown me. Amen.

79

Fear Is Not My Friend

—— *Suzanne* ——

I'm a fearful person by nature. I don't think Gretta knew the extent of my fear during our first semester of college, but she could probably tell a few stories about the resulting crazy perfection-driven behavior. I worried about earning the grades to keep my academic scholarship—a fear intensified by syllabus shock. So I undertook a frenzied pursuit of all *A*'s. Anything less felt like a threat to my future.

Over time, I learned to chill out (partly with Gretta's help) and not give fear so much control in my life. By the time I moved to Colorado after college for a job I loved, I didn't have many fears (other than being single forever). Then I got married and had my first child.

Talk about scary! First of all, the overabundance of baby advice convinces you that many, *many* things can go wrong with your child. What you feed your baby can affect her IQ. There is no perfectly safe way for your baby to sleep, so you better get the $300 breathing monitor, just in case. And car seats…if the straps are even a bit too loose, your baby could fly out in an accident; if they're a millimeter too high or too low, his organs could be crushed in a crash.

This would have been enough to induce a mild panic, but then something *did go wrong*. My baby ended up in the hospital with catastrophic seizures at seven months. My fears were no longer theoretical.

During the months where we weren't sure if he would get better, terror threatened to consume me.

Even after Josiah recovered from the immediate threats, fear lingered. A glance at my newsfeed revealed story after story of accidents and illnesses that planted seeds of fear about circumstances I had no control over. I became overwhelmed with all of the dangers that could befall my child.

Have you been there, Mama? Being a mommy can be scary business. I've often wondered if my mom had to deal with the same level of fear I do. I doubt it. She parented in simpler times. She didn't know about the friends-of-friends-of-friends (or strangers) whose child had cancer. She only knew about her friend—one other mama—whose son had cancer. She didn't have to stress over car seat safety—I mean, when I was a baby, she laid me at her feet to sleep during road trips. (It's a miracle I survived!) And baby advice was one book (instead of hundreds) about what to expect when you're expecting.

With seemingly endless possibilities of peril that could befall my child, I could easily be ruled by fear. But that's not how God wants me to live. Living in fear is futile, because I can't control what happens to my children. Plus, fear can prevent me from taking godly risks.

Second Timothy 1:7 reminds us that fear doesn't have to be a part of life with Christ: "For God gave us a spirit not of fear but of power and love and self-control" (ESV). As a child of God, fear doesn't have to be my default mode. My spirit is to be ruled by love, which casts out fear (1 John 4:18). More than that, I can place my confidence in God's power and take my fearful thoughts captive.

Even when our children are perfectly healthy and thriving, this world can be a scary place. And one day we will release them into the world to make their own decisions and take on their own challenges. But first we must release them to God. We won't always be right there to watch our children's every move or protect them, but God will be with them, just as He is right now.

Reining in fear requires self-control, reliance on God's power, and lots of love. When I realize that God loves my children even more than I do, I can release them into His care and not be afraid.

Lord, You know the fears I have for my children. Thank You that You have not given me the spirit of fear. I can be a bold mama as I experience Your love and power. Help me discipline my mind and heart to trust in You when I am afraid. Remind me that my children belong to You and are always under Your care. Amen.

80

Bedtime Lessons

——— *Gretta* ———

Bedtime has the potential to be some of the sweetest minutes of the entire day. When we had our sweet baby Kaia, all the books we read spoke about the importance of creating a peaceful routine for bedtime. So with lavender bath wash and baby massage oil in hand, we created an almost hour-long blissful routine. Every night she received a bath, a massage, singing, and some time nursing in the rocking chair before I gently laid her in her crib. It was heavenly.

By the time Titus arrived a year and a half later, we had bedtime dialed in. Adding one more to the mix certainly made it more challenging to keep up the peaceful routine, and when Koen joined our family shortly after, I'm pretty sure he was only bathed once a week or so while Kaia and Titus just got a rush job to lights out.

Before we knew what was happening, bedtime had morphed into a quick 20 minutes of reading, prayers, hugs, and kisses, "I love you. Good night." It became something to get done so that we could enjoy whatever remaining minutes of the day we could kid-free. It was no longer a connection point for cuddles. No sweetness. Just business. And boy, did everyone suffer. But I didn't notice the suffering at first. It started as a simple request for water, which turned into the need to go to the bathroom. Then the blankets needed fixing and the special stuffy went missing. Exasperated, my husband and I repeatedly visited each room to solve the problems, but we were frustrated, angry, and just *done*. I don't think it really had anything to do with having three kids. I think it had more to do with our desire for a break.

I read an article recently that said, "There are nine minutes during the day that can have the greatest impact on a child. The first three minutes—right after they wake up. The three minutes after they come home from school, and the last three minutes of the day—before they go to bed. We need to make those moments special and help our children feel loved."* Each of these three minutes are a vulnerable time when your child needs to connect and be reminded of their security with you. The more Jay and I rushed bedtime, the more the kids pushed back. Even at two and three years old, they knew we were trying to be done with them. Though it was for a good cause (our sanity), they were on to us. The crazy thing, though, is once we slowed down again, read the stories, took our time to snuggle, talked about the good and bad of the day, and prayed, we could turn out the light and walk away without fuss. And it was way more pleasant, less stressful, and above all deepened their security and our bonds as parent and child.

I'm just like my kids. I want to feel secure. I want to know God is available when I need or want Him. Perhaps that's why I love Psalm 121 so much.

> I lift my eyes to the hills—where does my help come from?
> My help comes from the LORD, the Maker of heaven and
> earth. He will not let your foot slip—he who watches over
> you will not slumber; indeed, he who watches over Israel
> will not slumber nor sleep (verses 1-4).

During every moment of my life, the God of the universe is available. He doesn't rush me off to bed or put me in a timeout. He's not trying to get time to Himself, and He is never done. He's actually the opposite of that. He's paying so close attention to you that He doesn't

---

* "Three Unbelievably Simple Parenting Ideas (That Work!)," Power of Moms, June 16, 2013, https://powerofmoms.com/mini-podcast-three-unbelievably-simple-ideas.

take a break for a quick slumber. That's how secure you are with God. Always available. Always ready and willing to help. Don't you need to know that? You don't have to be like my children and force all sorts of reasons to keep God's attention. You have it. So snuggle in—He's right there.

———————

God, thank You for being available always. I am thankful that You are watching over me so closely that You promise not to even let my foot slip. Remind me how I am secure with You and can always come to You with anything. Amen.

81

Simple Celebrations

—— *Suzanne* ——

He caught me in a weak moment. My three young children and I had just finished an early dinner and my husband wouldn't be home until late that evening. It was one of those Indian summer days in September, and I had been watching the clock for bedtime to arrive.

That's when Josiah said, "Mommy, it's the fan's birthday. Can we have a birthday party for the fan?" My son has had a fascination with fans since he was young. Whenever we enter a restaurant or store, he immediately finds any fans and points them out. When we video chat with Nana and Papa, he requests that they show him the fan in their house.

We had moved to California earlier that year, and Josiah had been delighted to discover a ceiling fan in every room of our new house. His favorite was the large ceiling fan in the center of our downstairs living room. I'm still not sure why he decided that it was the fan's birthday on this particular day. Perhaps some recent family celebrations prompted the idea. But I looked into my five-year-old's expectant eyes and couldn't say no. I agreed to throw a party for the fan.

My daughters squealed with excitement as they raced to the "birthday drawer" in search of paper plates and napkins for our party. They decorated and played with balloons while I prepared a box of brownies, which, full disclosure, I had been looking for an excuse to make. When the brownies were ready, I stood on a chair and placed a birthday hat on one of the fan's blades.

Josiah clapped his hands and laughed with glee. I asked the kids how old the fan was, and they said four. So we placed four candles in our brownies and sang happy birthday to the fan. Josiah helped the fan blow out its candles, and I cut a brownie square for each of us. Because of our impromptu party, a mundane day I thought would never end concluded on a sweet, festive note.

Celebration is a big theme throughout the Bible. When God laid out His specific instructions for Israel in the book of Exodus, He built in plenty of holidays, festivals, and feasts. It seems that celebration is to be a natural and regular part of our lives; God didn't design us to endure a dry, mundane existence. Celebration is part of the abundant life Jesus came to give us.

Listen to what Solomon says about this in Ecclesiastes 3:12-13:

> I know that there is nothing better for people than to be happy and to do good while they live. That each of them may eat and drink and find satisfaction in all their toil— this is the gift of God.

God has created us to enjoy Him and enjoy the things He has created. I imagine He smiles when He sees my little boy's love for fans. And I'm convinced He feels joy when my children appreciate the little things in life that come from Him.

So celebrate, Mama! It's okay. Take a picnic to the park to celebrate a beautiful afternoon. Throw a birthday party to honor a beloved stuffed animal. Declare a restful Saturday to be "PJs and Pancakes" day and put *all* the sprinkles on top of the whipped cream. These moments of celebration are gifts from God, and embracing them brings Him glory.

Psalm 126:3 proclaims, "The Lord has done great things for us, and we are filled with joy." Our celebration honors the God who gives us good gifts. That is a truth worth communicating to our children— even when it means having a party for a fan.

Lord, thank You for the gift of celebration. Because of Your goodness, we have so much to celebrate! Help me pause from my busyness and see the little moments that are worth throwing a party over. I pray that celebration would be a hallmark of our family and that it would cause us to turn our eyes toward You, the Giver of all good gifts. Amen.

82

Rainbows in the Bathroom

—— *Gretta* ——

"Mama, come quick! You have to see this. It's so beautiful!" They seem to know the very moment I sit down with a hot cup of coffee. I didn't want to "see this," but he was so insistent that I knew I needed to follow him to the bathroom.

The problem was we were headed to the kids-only bathroom. The very bathroom I try to avoid whenever possible because it's so filthy. Even if I manage to scrub it weekly, there is still toothpaste on the mirror, counter, and faucet. Young boys can't seem to aim properly, so the toilet area is a biohazard (seriously, boys, is it really that hard?). Semi-wet towels are strewn about the floor, and the built-in dirty laundry drawer is overflowing as usual. The floor itself is in desperate need of a mopping (or a chisel), and don't get me started on all the personal hygiene paraphernalia covering the counter. This room is downright disgusting. How do I let it get this bad? Oh, I know, there are a million other things crying (literally) for my attention all the livelong day. The kids' bathroom seems to consistently be among the last jobs on my priority list.

But today there was something beautiful I simply must come quickly to see. He was so proud to have found it, and the wonder on Koen's face was almost palpable. He stood there, gazing up at the sun streaming through the window—completely oblivious to the filth around him. I followed his gaze and saw it. As the sun's rays touched the shiny surface of the light fixture, little rainbows bounced about the room. On the dirty wall. On the dirty mirror. Koen stood there and said it again, "Mama, it's just so beautiful."

You know what's crazy? He was right. There's just something about shiny rainbow prisms that make everything a tad magical. My five-year-old was able to see what I couldn't—beauty.

Our lives are often like this bathroom. We are messy. We don't always say the right thing. We have broken relationships. Maybe painful pasts, hidden sins, addictions, or just plain ugly days. We want to look like we have it all together. We want to be the perfect wife. The fun mom. The listening friend. The one who fits into her prepregnancy clothes (face it, girl, your body's just different). But the reality is we are a mess. And when we try to do all this on our own, we just get messier.

But God, in His gentleness, is making us a new creation. He is at work in our lives, continually changing us into more of His likeness. He says in Ephesians 4:22-24, "You were taught…to be made new in the attitude of your minds; and to put on the new self, created to be like God in true righteousness and holiness." Then in the next chapter: "For you were once darkness, but now you are light in the Lord. Live as children of light (for the fruit of the light consists in all goodness, righteousness and truth)" (5:8-9).

See that? Good. And right. And true. Beautiful. That's God's work in your life. That's what people will see as you follow Him and are refined by Him.

Does this mean you won't still struggle? That all of the ugly patterns of behavior will instantly disappear? The quick answer is no. But the joy and hope is that you are being renewed and transformed. You are shining beauty, and little rainbows get to dance about you (figuratively of course). *That's* what others see. And they will call it beautiful. God's light in you. Good. Right. And true.

———

God, help me see Your beauty in my life. Sometimes
I'm overwhelmed by the mess and the ugly parts of

me. But help me focus on the work You are doing and how You are making me a new creation day by day. Help me radiate Your rainbows so that others will see that beauty because of You. Amen.

83

Better Together

—— *Suzanne* ——

Our first major road trip with young children almost ended in disaster. We decided to take a road trip from Colorado to Washington State with three children four and under. I know that sounds like the punch line, but there's more.

The first day started out great. We left the house by 5:30 and made it north of Denver traffic by seven. That's when the "fun" began. Our two-year-old started to whimper, and before we could find an exit, she got sick. All over her clothes and blanket. We stopped at a gas station and used about half a package of wipes and changed her clothes. I was pretty proud of how quickly and efficiently we took care of the problem. Thanks to a plastic bag and wipes, the car didn't even smell that bad.

Ten hours later, we pulled into Billings, Montana, to meet a friend for dinner. When I opened the van door, I realized our one-year-old had experienced a similar "event." We used the rest of the wipes and quickly changed her into a clean outfit.

After dinner, we hit the road for our final two hours before reaching the hotel. Baby Amelia was wailing inconsolably, so I switched seats to sit next to her in the back. Thinking she was hungry, I fed her two pear-spinach pouches. About 20 minutes later, two pear-spinach pouches came back up. (Conveniently her car seat was green!)

We got to the hotel at ten with three exhausted children, two soiled car seats, and about half a dozen loads of stuff to carry up a flight of stairs to our room. I was beginning to wonder if we had made an epic mistake attempting a road trip with three young children. But an hour later we were settled in and Kevin headed to the laundry room while I attempted to quiet the children in their beds. I've already talked about what happened next (see page 210), but let's just say, I did not pass the stress test.

However, Kevin did. He simply did what had to be done. In this case, that meant sitting in the laundry room until 2:00 a.m. until the seats, straps, buckles, and soiled clothes had been washed. The next morning I watched him painstakingly put the seats back together before we could leave. We then drove through Yellowstone National Park and had a lovely time.

As I recall how those stressful events almost ruined our vacation, I'm reminded of how God shows up in families. Talking about the family of believers, Paul writes,

> Just as each of us has one body with many members, and these members do not all have the same function, so in Christ we, though many, form one body, and each member belongs to all the others (Romans 12:4-5).

The same is true of my family, which is a microcosm of the greater family of God.

Each member is different and possesses different strengths and weaknesses. We belong to each other. And as we exercise the gifts and strengths God has given us, we bless the entire body and even the world.

There are many things I appreciate about my husband, but near the top of the list is this ability he has to handle stressful situations— keeping a positive outlook and not giving up. This quality, which was instilled in him by his parents, is a huge blessing to our family, especially during this demanding season of life. I possess different strengths— such as discernment in the midst of challenges, an ability to ask good questions, and a knack for talking to my kids about God. I love seeing how God uses Kevin and me together to lead our children and point them to Him.

Our vacation wasn't ruined. In fact, it only got better from there. And as we learn to work together as a family, our lives and experiences will only get better as well. Then, when our best-laid plans come tumbling down around us, we can stay calm, pick up the pieces, and move forward...together.

———————

Lord, I realize I am not meant to handle all that life throws at me on my own. I praise You for showing up in all the chaos and stress of life. Thank You for my family and most of all for Your unfailing presence. Help us reflect Your purposes as we work together, using our individual gifts and strengths to serve You. Amen.

84

The Sneaky Rodent

—— *Gretta* ——

Occasionally Jay and I like to watch a movie after we put the kids to bed. Okay, it's more than occasionally, as movie watching is our go-to way to relax and unwind. Our kids sleep upstairs and our family room is down, so one night after they were asleep, we settled in for a relaxing evening. Winter was upon us, the fire blazed in our family room, and with the lights turned off and the TV turned on, we snuggled on the couch. It was quite cozy.

About halfway into the movie I heard a noise in the kitchen directly next to us. But since the dishwasher was running, I didn't think too much of it. A few minutes later I thought I saw something move from the corner of my eye. With the lights off it was hard to tell if my peripheral vision was playing tricks on me or not, so without alerting Jay I just kept more careful attention to the kitchen than to the movie. Moments later my eyes were certain and I shouted, "A rat! A rat! A rat! Jay, there's a rat in the kitchen!"

Now, you need to know that we live in a town where huge ships come into port from all over and they carry with them…rats. Plus, we live in the country with 30 chickens. Rats, sadly, are inevitable. However, we had never had one venture into our living space like this before.

Jay flew off the cozy couch, I flipped on the lights, and for the next five minutes we chased our new unwanted pet around the kitchen. He eventually scurried back under the stove and lived for the following week between the stove and the dishwasher. We barricaded the area, found how he got in, and sealed that off too. We could hear him scratch every night as he tried to break free, but alas, he was stuck.

I don't know what exactly we were trying to accomplish by keeping him sequestered. He wasn't eating, but he sure started stinking. It didn't take long for his bathroom smells to make their way through the dishwasher. I no longer put dirty dishes in there because I felt they would just come out smelling worse than before they went in.

We realized we needed to get this rodent out from under the cupboards and exterminate him. It took patience and diligence, but eventually he came out. We spent the next 20 minutes trying to capture him. Let me just say I had no idea rats could jump four feet in the air! We used a combination of an eight-foot table turned on its side, a cardboard box, a garbage bag, and a hockey stick (hey, we live in Canada, remember?) and finally we caught our rat.

It never occurred to us to allow the rat to live in our home. It would be ridiculous. Rats carry diseases, they poo everywhere, and if they get into the food (which is inevitable), you have to throw it all out. Instead, we rid our home of it, and once the rat was gone, I washed and sterilized everything I could that he had touched, including all the toys he ran around and behind while being chased with a hockey stick.

The rat is a reminder of everything Paul said to run from and get out of our lives. Colossians 3:8 says, "But now you must rid yourselves of all such things as these: anger, rage, malice, slander, and filthy language from your lips." And in Ephesians 4:31 he adds to the list bitterness and brawling.

You see, if we hold on to these destructive behaviors and patterns, it will be as though we allow the rat to live in our lives, stinking up the place, and not only making us sick, but keeping others from us as well. Take a look at that list. Where do you struggle? Do you hold on to your anger and bitterness? Do you speak poorly of others? Does your pride prevent you from getting along with some people around you?

I gotta tell you, there is good news. God never asks you to get rid of something without telling you what to replace it with. He never leaves us empty. He says to replace these destructive behaviors with compassion, kindness, humility, gentleness, patience, forgiveness, and love. Yes, that's a big list, but the only way you can put on all that is through God's help as He continually renews you into the image of Christ. As you press into God's Word and open yourself to His transforming power, the rats in your life will be exterminated.

———————

Lord, I can see that I've allowed rats to live in my home for far too long. I struggle with _____. Please, with Your transforming power, will You replace that with all the life-giving behaviors that You ask me to have instead? Help me change and rid the rat from my life. Amen.

85

I Just Want to Be with You

———— Suzanne ————

I hear the familiar squeak of my bedroom door and a little blonde head peeks around the corner. Kevin and I are in bed chatting, preparing to go to bed early. And like a scene from *The Brady Bunch*, our three-year-old scuttles over to the side of our bed.

"What do you need, Amelia?" Kevin asks.

She purses her lips and crinkles her forehead. "I just want to be with you," she says.

She's good.

And I know her bedtime ploys all too well. But this goes beyond her ordinary request for a snack or water. So I let her climb up. She settles contentedly between Kevin and me and sighs happily.

It reminds me of a time a few months earlier when we were listening to Christmas music and Mariah Carey's classic "All I Want for Christmas Is You" played. Amelia was sitting at the kitchen table while I did dishes. She paused from what she was doing and looked up.

"All I want for Christmas is *you*," she said, looking directly into my eyes. She smiled and resumed her coloring, but her words went deep into my heart. I knew immediately that what she'd said was more than the words of a song. And I felt the weight again of the beautiful responsibility I've been given.

Maybe that's why, months later when she makes her bedtime appearance, we invite her in and chat with her about her day. The other three kids are asleep, and this is a rare moment with our middle child. She tells us what is important to her young heart, which mainly revolves around childish imaginings and her toys. As we sit there, I will my rule-following side to ignore the fact that it's after nine and this angel-girl should be sleeping. I let her nestle in and revel in the joy of our company.

The moment reminded me of my relationship with my heavenly Father. Do I want to be with Him the way my daughter wants to be with me? Is He my top desire? Do I long to sit with Him each day?

After He calls the church at Laodicea to earnestly repent for being lukewarm in its spiritual passion, Jesus says these words in Revelation 3:20: "Here I am! I stand at the door and knock. If anyone hears my voice and opens the door, I will come in and eat with that person, and they with me."

How amazing that Jesus does the knocking! He is waiting for me to open the door and enjoy one-on-one fellowship with the Creator and Ruler of the universe. He longs for intimate communion with me. When I peek around that door, He is always pleased to see me. He wants to be with *me*.

Too often I forego the intimacy with Jesus and the Father that is available to me. I allow myself to desire other things such as comfort and prestige that will never truly make me happy. All the while, my Father is waiting for me to come to Him. He's waiting to hear these words: "I just want to be with You."

Sitting with God daily requires discipline and desire. First, I must discipline myself to set aside my to-do list and the worries of the day long enough to read God's Word and respond. Second, I must feed my desire for Him by turning my thoughts to Him over and over again. The more time I spend in His presence, the more I will crave it.

Amelia snuggles her head against my shoulder. "Aw, Mama," she breathes out with delight. "I just want to be with you." I tell her I hope she always feels that way—even when she's 25. And I commit anew to spending time with my gracious, good, and loving Father.

Lord, thank You for pursuing me with Your reckless love. Thank You that while I was helpless in my sin, You died for me and made a way for me to have a relationship with You. I am forever grateful. Help me to exult in Your presence like a child. Give me greater passion for You today. Amen.

86

Stone by Stone

———— *Gretta* ————

One night I was reading out of Nehemiah with Kaia before she went to sleep. I could still smell her freshly shampooed hair as she lay next to me on the bed. Reading together is one of my daughter's favorite activities, though usually we read from a children's Bible instead of the grown-up version. Since I couldn't find our regular Bible, I picked up mine and thought I'd start in Nehemiah. Yes, odd, but I knew the story and was expecting lots of action and intriguing details to discuss with her. You know, building a great wall in record time with God's help and all that. As it turns out, the story wasn't as exciting as I remembered. Three chapters in, I found myself tempted to switch books, realizing I might have a hard time figuring out what kind of application this passage could have for us.

I plodded on, stumbling through fairly boring details about who rebuilt each section of the wall surrounding Jerusalem and struggling to say names such as Hashabneiah, Azbuk, and Binnui. (If you're looking for unique baby names, I'm sure you can find one here. You may not be able to pronounce it, but no one else in your son's preschool class will have it!)

When I got to the end of the chapter, I was sure Kaia would be asleep. I asked the question anyway. "Honey, what was going on in the story?"

"I don't know," she replied, "but they had a lot of funny names back then."

"Why do you suppose God wanted us to read all of those different-sounding names?" I asked, hoping God would direct the conversation so I didn't feel like I had wasted our Bible time.

"I guess because those people mattered." She said it so matter-of-factly. But lying on her bed, I was struck by a truth I wasn't expecting to hear and one I often forget. All the people matter. These Israelites, who had returned from exile in a foreign land, had a great task ahead of them: to rebuild the wall surrounding Jerusalem that lay in ruins. Each of them did their part—the part right in front of their home. They had no way of knowing that their obedience and hard work would be recorded for a mom and daughter to read about 3,000 years later. They were just doing the hard work before them. Stone by stone. Obedient to God.

How many stones have you placed today? How many toys have you picked up? How many diapers have you changed? How many hours of sleep have you lost because your baby is teething and needs extra cuddles? It's hard work doing the daily tasks in front of you. But God sees you. You matter.

You are building into God's kingdom with each seemingly insignificant task you do. Those actions add up. And God sees you. As I read back over those hard-to-pronounce names after my daughter was sleeping peacefully, I saw something beautiful. No one was given the task of rebuilding the entire wall by themselves. That would be impossible. Instead, everyone was faithful to do the bit entrusted to them for that day.

You have been entrusted with your child. Sometimes if we look at the whole task of raising them to adulthood, it can feel daunting. But God has just asked you to be faithful with today. He sees you as you build into your child's identity and faith through each small act of service. He is pleased as you seek to obey the calling He gave you when you became a mother. Today, as you faithfully place one stone on top of another in obedience, may you understand that your work matters more than you know.

―――――――

Lord, help me be faithful with the tasks of today. Keep my eyes focused on the "now" and remind me of my value and worth in the process. Give me sustenance to keep going when I'm tired, and encourage me with the truth that You are using my obedience to build something eternal into my children. Amen.

87

The Truth About Moms

—— Suzanne ——

A few years ago, during an exhausting season of being at home with three young children, I read some good news. A coffee chain I like was planning to test market delivery services in some areas of the country.

I quickly posted what I thought was a funny comment on the online news article saying that as a stay-at-home mom of toddlers, I was in favor of the idea. Minutes later, my comment had garnered dozens of responses, most of them negative. After being called "stupid," "lazy," "a bad parent," and "a person who makes stay-at-home-moms look bad," I deleted my comment.

To say I felt misunderstood would be an understatement. I've been around the Internet long enough to have grown a fairly thick skin. But these comments were like a fiery arrow to my mama heart. *Am I lazy?* I thought. *Am I a terrible person? Do I make other SAHMs look bad?*

As I was trying to fall asleep that night, insecurities and doubts swirled through my mind. I wondered what kind of pain those people had experienced that would motivate them to spew such hateful words toward a total stranger. Maybe they were simply picking a fight for the entertainment value. Either way, God impressed something on my heart: *They don't get it.*

We live in a world that doesn't always value motherhood the way God does. I can feel a lot of pressure to "prove myself" as a mom so that others will know that I didn't make a mistake bringing these littles into the world. The other message I regularly receive is that being a mama takes something away from me—having children stalls my career, ruins my body, stresses my marriage, and drains my bank account.

Seldom do people talk about all the things I gain from being a mom. Love beyond description in the form of sticky kisses and toddlers who can't even bear to be parted from me when I have to use the bathroom. Watching my children giggle and play together. Or seeing them do the right thing and feeling such joy that I think my heart will burst. Not to mention the eternal legacy I have through my kids. God has plans to use them for His glory.

Being a mom is a high calling and a challenge. Whether you're a working mama or you stay home with your kids, you don't have it easy. Listen to this encouragement for mamas found in a well-worn passage of Scripture:

> She is clothed with strength and dignity; she can laugh at the days to come. She speaks with wisdom, and faithful instruction is on her tongue. She watches over the affairs of her household and does not eat the bread of idleness. Her children arise and call her blessed; her husband also, and he praises her. "Many women do noble things, but you surpass them all" (Proverbs 31:25-29).

At times I've viewed that passage as an impossible checklist. Let's face it, living up to the standards of the mythical Proverbs 31 woman is daunting. She's like the unicorn of moms. But read the passage again. Are you giving your children faithful instruction? Are you watching over the affairs of your home? I already know you're a strong woman. You have to be to care for young children.

Now look at the honor that shines from this passage. Her children rise up and call her blessed. Her husband praises her. Her nobility causes her to stand out.

When I took to social media to share what had happened, my

friends came swiftly and strongly to my defense. One of my favorite comments was this: "All moms are working moms—it is just our work-place that is different. Our hours go from 7 a.m. to 7 a.m. and even if we are 'on vacation' we are at work! Someone who would call a mom lazy for wanting delivery obviously has no idea the amount of work it takes to get small children ready and out the door."

Stay the course, Mama. Being misunderstood pales in comparison to hearing their sweet little calls—"Mom, look at this"…"Mom, I love you"…"Mom, I need you." Take advantage of each moment.

——————

Lord, thank You for the incredible privilege of being a mom. Thank You for calling me to this work and equipping me for it. Remind me today that what I am doing matters and that You are with me. Amen.

88

A Bit of Brain Power

———— Gretta ————

"Mama, have you ever heard of the myelin sheath?"

"Why no, buddy, I have no idea what you're talking about. What is it?"

He then proceeded to tell me about a fiber in the brain that builds up around memories and actions. The fibers create a sheath around the memory, concept, idea, thought, or action, strengthening it over time. Titus lit up as he described the myelin sheath to me. He thought it was pretty cool that he was turning into the teacher and I was the student. But mostly he was in awe of how God had created the brain. As we repeat behaviors and thoughts, really anything, the sheath builds up stronger and stronger to protect and solidify the electrical currents of those behaviors and thoughts. Then, all on his own, Titus linked something (yeah, I'm pretty sure he's a genius).

"Mom, I've been thinking for a while about why we have to keep reading the same Bible stories over and over. I keep thinking that I've heard the story, so why read it again? But now I know it's because of the myelin sheath! I have to keep reading it so I won't ever forget the parts of the story!"

Oh. My. Word. This kid is so right. Immediately my mind went to God's commissioning of Joshua right before he led the Israelites into the promised land. God tells Joshua, "Keep this Book of the Law always on your lips; meditate on it day and night, so that you may be... prosperous and successful" (Joshua 1:8). Meditate, God says, day and night. Think on the law. Stew on it. Roll it over in your mind, over and over, so you will strengthen that myelin sheath and never forget God's law.

Our brains are powerful. If they weren't, we wouldn't be given so much instruction about how to use them. Philippians 4:8 says,

> Finally, brothers and sisters, whatever is true, whatever is noble, whatever is right, whatever is pure, whatever is lovely, whatever is admirable—if anything is excellent or praiseworthy—think about such things.

These words give us so much encouragement for how to live. God tells us what to think about because He knows our brains are powerful tools. Science is proving what God created to be true from the beginning of time. In a study done by King's College, people who suffer from anxiety disorders were asked to visualize a positive image whenever they started to worry. They found that just thinking positively lowered their anxiety and gave them greater happiness and restfulness, thus influencing their behaviors.

The reverse is true as well. Negative thinking leads to more stress, restlessness, and dissatisfaction. Have you noticed this to be true in your life? In mine it works like this: I get frustrated with my husband and feel he's not doing enough to help around the house. Then I start looking for examples to prove my idea, and in just a few days (or even minutes), my attitude is rotten toward him. The longer I hold those thoughts, the more my perception of his character changes. I become resentful and angry and think the worst of him. That negative thought, when fed over time, will build strength and create a rift between the two of us.

But if I take that same scenario and adjust my thinking to what Philippians 4:8 says, it will take a whole different spin. I may still feel my husband doesn't help out enough around the house, but I will see him come home and hold our baby girl and bond with her. I will recognize the long hours he puts in at work to provide for our young family. As those good and true thoughts roll around in my mind, my love for him grows and my relationship deepens.

Our mind holds incredible power, and we get to control what we spend our time dwelling on. The wise woman will listen to God's command and build up her myelin sheath on things that are:

1. True (not the sneaky lies of Satan)
2. Noble (like a trustworthy, good king)
3. Right
4. Pure (without fault or blemish)
5. Lovely (the tender thoughts of life)
6. Admirable (what we aspire to)

And in thinking like that, she will influence not only her life but the lives of everyone she meets. So what do you say? Isn't it time to switch thinking and build your myelin sheath accordingly?

———————

God, You gave me a powerful brain and I don't always
use it the way You have designed. Help me think on
things that are from You and beneficial to both myself
and those around me. I want to honor You with my mind
and build the strength of the good thoughts. Amen.

89

Unexpected Gifts

—— *Suzanne* ——

Our day had started out a little rough. I'd been the sole person responsible for getting my four young children ready for Sunday-morning service. We usually attend the evening service when my husband, who is a pastor, can help us get out the door. But a last-minute schedule change had forced us to go in the morning.

And so I arrived to the elementary building a bit frazzled, remembering that I'd forgotten to line up a "buddy" for seven-year-old Josiah, who has special needs. I dropped him off in a first-grade class he never attends, hastily explaining the situation to the teacher. She said it would be fine, and I headed over to the service, hoping she was right.

When worship was over, I walked back to Josiah's classroom to pick him up. "Mommy!" he yelled, flashing his Jack-o-lantern grin and jumping up and down with excitement.

"How was church?" I asked.

"Great!" he said, offering his standard answer. My son's enthusiasm is definitely one of his most endearing qualities.

At that moment, the children's director came over. "His teacher had to leave early," she said, "but she wanted me to tell you that Josiah was a blessing to her today. She said she had started the day in a funk, and he was just what she needed."

These words were extra meaningful to me because of our journey with our oldest child. I was never angry at God for giving us a special needs child, but I did wonder sometimes how Josiah would fit into God's plan. He wouldn't do some of the "normal" things we had imagined, and I didn't even know how he would come to have a relationship with Jesus. Yet we still firmly believed Josiah, like all of our children, was a gift from the Lord.

Psalm 127:3 says it well: "Behold, children are a gift of the Lord, the fruit of the womb is a reward" (NASB). Some other versions use the word *heritage*, which can be defined as "a special or individual possession; an allotted portion." Children aren't just a moderately good thing, they are a *reward*. They are an inheritance.

I remember having a conversation with a mom of teens while I was still single. Her sons were polite and considerate, and I complimented her on their behavior. "Well," she said, "my husband and I prayed that our children would be a delight to others. And we tried to raise them that way." Her words stuck with me many years later when I was pregnant with our first child.

I think having children that are a delight to others is a wonderful goal. But more than that, I want my children to be a gift—vessels God uses to accomplish His purposes. And that may not always look the way I think it should.

After church was over that Sunday, my husband received two text messages from others who said that Josiah had been an answer to prayer by being in that classroom that morning. I marveled at how we almost had not come to that service and how God had used my lack of preparedness to give that teacher a gift—the gift of a joyful child who thinks and acts differently than most first graders. A child who declares the glory of God in his own way and is not defined by a diagnosis but as a special creation of God. When I catch these glimpses of God working in ways so far outside of my thoughts and comprehension, all I can do is praise Him for His magnificent ways.

Psalm 139:5-6 says, "You lay your hand upon me. Such knowledge is too wonderful for me, too lofty for me to attain." Your children are a gift, a special allotment. And God's hand is on you, Mama. Even if that child has a different personality or functionality than you antic-ipated, God has a plan for it all. Every bit. He will work in ways you could never imagine.

———————

Lord, thank You for the gift of my child. Thank You for knowing better than I do who that little one will one day be. I praise You for the ways You are already using my children for Your glory. Thank You that Your hand is on me. Help me to be sensitive to Your spirit and how You are working in and through my family. Amen.

90

It Happened

———— Gretta ————

I was out with my family at a park enjoying a picnic lunch when my three children ran over to the playground to burn off some energy. As I watched them play, I heard myself call out to them, "Be careful to look out for the little ones. You guys are much bigger than the other kids around you."

It happened. Everyone said it would. My children are no longer the youngest ones when we go places. There are no middle-of-the-night feedings, no diapers, no formula or baby food mush. My babies are now kids who go to school and who can communicate with words and use the bathroom unassisted. When did this happen?

Because our three kids were born in under three years, I spent many days in a dark tunnel. After giving birth to Koen, it occurred to me that Titus had only been walking for three months and Kaia had been out of diapers for just a few months herself. To say my hands were full is an understatement. The days were hard. The days were long. That's the tunnel I was in. I couldn't see anything except the immediate and demanding needs of the children in front of me.

My days were exhausting, and I didn't feel I had anything to show for my exhaustion other than the fact that the humans were all still alive. People told me this wouldn't last forever, that it's only a season.

These people meant well, but when I was covered in spit-up it was hard to believe.

Then my sister-in-law said that phrase mentioned at the beginning of the book: "The days are long, but the years are short." That phrase became one of my dear mantras. It's what I held on to in order to get through those really long days. I knew one day I would wonder where the time went.

Mothering is just like Ecclesiastes 3:1: "There is a time for everything, and a season for every activity under the heavens." The following verses go on to describe all the different seasons, like the old Simon and Garfunkel song, "a time to be born and a time to die…" But after watching my no-longer-babies playing at the park, I am tempted to rewrite the following verses of chapter 3: a time to breastfeed and a time to feed yourself, a time to be diapered and a time to use the toilet, a time to crawl and a time to run, a time to babble and a time to speak full, cohesive sentences, a time to scribble and a time to write down your own stories, a time to be rocked and a time to put yourself to bed, a time for car seats and a time for sitting in the front seat.

Yes, this is what happened to me when I recognized how big they had grown. Now the days fly by, and I can't believe how the seasons change. Ecclesiastes is right. There really is a time and season for everything. We see it in nature, and we see it in our home too. There is a temptation to sometimes want relief from the season we are in so that we look ahead to the next one before it's time. While that can work when it comes to wanting spring when we are experiencing winter, it's dangerous when looking at our families. With nature, we can always return to winter; we just need to wait a few months for it to come back. But with our children, they will never be babies, toddlers, and pre-schoolers again. If we spend all our time wishing they would grow, we will miss the greatness of these demanding years.

Well-meaning women often told me when the kids were tiny to "enjoy every moment because it goes so fast." I'd smile, but inside think, *I'm sorry, but no. I will not enjoy every moment. Especially when my daughter just ruined all my new makeup and my son decided to repaint the bedroom with nail polish!* So I decided to take a different stance. I decided to savor the moments. I decided to start taking more pictures of the mess and the chaos, because there is a time and a season to everything and I would never get these moments back. It definitely helped me keep a better perspective. And that's what Ecclesiastes 3 is talking about. Life is not stagnant. It changes constantly, so be prepared for it. And savor the moments.

———————

God, thank You for my family. Even when the moments get crazy and beyond fun, help me savor my moments, remembering they will change tomorrow. Even when the kids try my patience, remind me that this is a season and I will never get it back. Help me see these demanding days as a blessing and to rejoice in the crazy. Amen.

Acknowledgments

—— From Suzanne ——

I would like to thank my husband, Kevin, who champions my dreams and enables me to use my talents both inside and outside the home. You are the one my soul loves and my favorite coffee date—I am so very thankful for you.

Thank you to my children, Josiah, Sadie, Amelia, and Jackson, who provided ample inspiration for this book. You teach me every day about the Father's deep, unconditional love for me. And you're some of the coolest humans I know.

To my parents and siblings, who showed me what it means to be an imperfect family loving Jesus and growing in grace. I see now how blessed I was to grow up among you—in a place full of fun, love, and laughter. You have never stopped encouraging me, and I thank God for you!

To my husband's family, whom I have only known for one short decade, you have blessed me, and us, in countless ways and are an important part of our lives. I could not have asked for a better or kinder support system.

To Carol, an extraordinary and beloved babysitter. When people ask me how I wrote a book with four young children in the house, my answer is, "Carol." Every warrior mama needs a good babysitter, and we are blessed to have you.

Thank you to my college roommate, friend, and coauthor, Gretta. When God made you my roommate, I received something precious. As different as we are, you were—and are—the perfect friend for me. Little did we know that God would one day give us the same dream to encourage other mamas.

Thank you to my editor and friend, Kathleen Kerr. Though we have worked on many projects together, this is the first time I've had the opportunity to officially thank you. You encouraged this project from the start, and I am so grateful for your investment. Never forget that what you are doing is changing lives.

Thank you to Betty, Jessica, and the rest of the team at Harvest House. You have been exceedingly gracious, and it is a joy to work with you.

Most of all, thank You, Jesus. You are my hope and salvation. Thank You for allowing me to live out my dream of being a mother. You have done great things, and I praise You for all of them.

A huge thank you to my dear husband, Jay. Without your unending encouragement, I never would have had the courage to attempt writing a book. I love learning and growing together and pray our home will forever honor our Savior. I choose you today and always.

To my three precious gifts, Kaia, Titus, and Koen. Thank you for giving me my favorite name ever…mama. God continues to use you three to teach me about love, grace, and patience. I pray you follow God with your whole heart and are mighty warriors for him. I love you to the moon.

Thank you to my parents, Dwight and Sarah, for teaching me what it looks like to be a woman of grit and grace. Thank you for giving me the gift of a Christ-centered home and modeling a loving marriage.

Thank you to my husband's parents, Clayton and Marlene, for your support, care, generosity, and for your faithful dedication to all of us.

To Suzanne, my dear friend, this book is a testament to God's incredibly gracious work in both of us. I am encouraged by the depth of our conversations and how you always point us back to God's Word.

Thank you to our editor, Kathleen Kerr, for your immense encouragement and patience with me as I dove into uncharted waters.

And my deepest gratitude belongs to my Savior, Jesus Christ. He knows me more fully than I can ever imagine and still, because of His unfailing love, He chooses to call me His own. Thank You, Lord, for allowing me to be a wife and mother. I am blown away by Your gracious love, Your immense holiness, and Your unfathomable forgiveness. I will praise You forever!